Contents

INDEX ON CENSORSHIP
VOLUME 44 NUMBER 03
AUTUMN 2015

Special report

Spies, secrets and lies: how yesterday's and today's censors compare

In focus

Culture

EDITOR
Rachael Jolley
DEPUTY EDITOR
Vicky Baker
SUB EDITORS
Sean Anderson, Alex Dudok de Wit, Sally Gimson, Tom Wein, Robin Wilson
CONTRIBUTING EDITORS:
Kaya Genç (Turkey), Natasha Joseph (South Africa), Jemimah Steinfeld, Irene Caselli

EDITORIAL ASSISTANT
Max Goldbart
DESIGN
Matthew Hasteley
COVER
Ben Jennings
THANKS TO:
Jodie Ginsberg, Sean Gallagher, Milana Knezevic, Small Media, Hamid Ismailov, Robert Chandler

Magazine printed by Page Bros., Norwich, UK

index on censorship

Supported by ARTS COUNCIL ENGLAND

Index on Censorship, 92-94 Tooley Street, London SE1 2TH, United Kingdom

Spies in the new machines

EDITORIAL

44(03): 3/5 | DOI: 10.1177/0306422015605693

by **Rachael Jolley**

IN THE OLD days governments kept tabs on "intellectuals", "subversives", "enemies of the state" and others they didn't like much by placing policemen in the shadows, across from their homes. These days writers and artists can find government spies inside their computers, reading their emails, and trying to track their movements via use of smart phones and credit cards.

Post-Soviet Union, after the fall of the Berlin wall, after the Bosnian war of the 1990s, and after South Africa's apartheid, the world's mood was positive. Censorship was out, and freedom was in.

But in the world of the new censors, governments continue to try to keep their critics in check, applying pressure in all its varied forms. Threatening, cajoling and propaganda are on one side of the corridor, while spying and censorship are on the other side at the Ministry of Silence. Old tactics, new techniques.

While advances in technology – the arrival and growth of email, the wider spread of the web, and access to computers – have aided individuals trying to avoid censorship, they have also offered more power to the authorities.

There are some clear examples to suggest that governments are making sure technology is on their side. The Chinese government has just introduced a new national security law to aid closer control of internet use. Virtual private networks have been used by citizens for years as tunnels through the Chinese government's Great Firewall for years. So it is no wonder that China wanted to close them down, to keep information under control. In the last few months more people in China are finding their VPN is not working.

Meanwhile in South Korea, new legislation means telecommunication companies are forced to put software inside teenagers' mobile phones to monitor and restrict their access to the internet.

Both these examples suggest that technological advances are giving all the winning censorship cards to the overlords.

But it is not as clear cut as that. People continually find new ways of tunnelling through firewalls, and getting messages out and in. As new apps are designed, other opportunities arise. For example, Telegram is an app, that allows the user to put a timer on each message, after which it detonates and disappears. New auto-encrypted email services, such as Mailpile, look set to take off. Now geeks among you may argue that they'll be a record somewhere, but each advance is a way of making it more difficult to be intercepted. With more than six billion people now using mobile phones around the world, it should be easier than ever before to get the word out in some form, in some way.

When Writers and Scholars International, the parent group to Index, was formed in 1972, its founding committee wrote that it was paradoxical that "attempts to nullify the artist's vision and to thwart the →

RIGHT: Drone pilots use virtual reality goggles to steer their machines around obstacles, and record information. Seen here at a UK competition

Credit: Jon Super/Rex

→ communication of ideas, appear to increase proportionally with the improvement in the media of communication".

And so it continues.

When we cast our eyes back to the Soviet Union, when suppression of freedom was part of government normality, we see how it drove its vicious idealism through using subversion acts, sedition acts, and allegations of anti-patriotism, backed up with imprisionment, hard labour, internal deportation and enforced poverty. One of those thousands who suffered was the satirical writer Mikhail Zoshchenko, who was a Russian WWI hero who was later denounced in the Zhdanov decree of 1946. This condemned all artists whose work didn't slavishly follow government lines. We publish a poetic tribute to Zoshchenko written by Lev Ozerov in this issue. The poem echoes some of the issues faced by writers in Russia today.

And so to Azerbaijan in 2015, a member of the Council of Europe (a body described by one of its founders as "the conscience of Europe"), where writers, artists, thinkers and campaigners are being imprisoned for having the temerity to advocate more freedom, or to articulate ideas that are different from those of their government. And where does Russia sit now? Journalists Helen Womack and Andrei Aliaksandrau write in this issue of new propaganda techniques and their fears that society no longer wants "true" journalism.

Plus ça change

When you compare one period with another, you find it is not as simple as it was bad then, or it is worse now. Methods are different, but the intention is the same. Both old censors and new censors operate in the hope that they can bring more silence. In Soviet times there was a bureau that gave newspapers a stamp of approval. Now in Russia journalists report that self-censorship is one of the greatest threats to the free flow of ideas and information. Others say the public's appetite for investigative journalism that challenges the authorities has disappeared. Meanwhile Vladamir Putin's government has introduced bills banning "propaganda" of homosexuality and promoting "extremism" or "harm to children", which can be applied far and wide to censor articles or art that the government doesn't like. So far, so familiar.

Censorship and threats to freedom of expression still come in many forms as they did in 1972. Murder and physical violence, as with the killings of bloggers in Bangladesh, tries to frighten other writers, scholars, artists and thinkers into silence, or exile. Imprisonment (for example, the six year and three month sentence of democracy campaigner Rasul Jafarov in Azerbaijan) attempts to enforces silence too. Instilling fear by breaking into individuals' computers and tracking their movement (as one African writer reports to Index) leaves a frightening signal that the government knows what you do and who you speak with.

Also in this issue, veteran journalist Andrew Graham-Yool looks back at Argentina's dictatorship of four decades ago, he argues that vicious attacks on journalists' reputations are becoming more widespread and he identifies numerous threats on the horizon, from corporate control of journalistic stories to the power of the president, Cristina Fernández de Kirchner, to identify journalists as enemies of the state.

Old censors and new censors have more in common than might divide them. Their intentions are the same, they just choose different weapons. Comparisons should make it clear, it remains ever vital to be vigilant for attacks on free expression, because they come from all angles.

Old and new censors have more in common than might divide them. Their intentions are the same, they just choose different weapons

Despite this, there is hope. In this issue of the magazine Jamie Bartlett writes of his optimism that when governments push their powers too far, the public pushes back hard, and gains ground once more. Another of our writers Jason DaPonte identifies innovators whose aim is to improve freedom of expression, bringing open-access software and encryption tools to the global public.

Don't miss our excellent new creative writing, published for the first time in English, including Russian poetry, an extract of a Brazilian play, and a short story from Turkey.

As always the magazine brings you brilliant new writers and writing from around the world. Read on.

***Rachael Jolley** is editor of Index on Censorship magazine. Follow the magazine on Twitter @ index_magazine. If you would like to join us at magazine launch debates and events, please email: davidh@indexoncensorship.org*

Credit: Steve Meddle/Rex

SPECIAL REPORT

Spies, secrets and lies: how yesterday's and today's censors compare

MAIN: Times and spying tools have changed since this Enigma machine was used at Bletchley Park, England, during World War II

New dog, old tricks

44(03): 8/13 | DOI: 10.1177/0306422015605694

With the internet in China recently coming under even greater restriction and loopholes continually being closed, **Jemimah Steinfeld** compares life and censorship in 1980s China with today, and explores the ongoing battle of wits with the regime's guardians

LEFT: A man stands in front of a house where revolutionary slogans are painted in Dongzhai village, Guangxi Zhuang, China. The village is known locally for its revolutionary slogans dating from the 1950s. The slogan on this wall reads: "Learn from the supreme instructions, execute the supreme instructions, promote the supreme instructions and defend the supreme instructions"

Credit: Reuters/Stringer

WEIWEI, A CHINESE journalist, insisted on only communicating with Index via the social media app Telegram. "It's safer than Facebook and Weibo," he said, and not tapped like his phone. His messages vanished almost as soon as they appeared. Weiwei had set a timer, which automatically removed them after a minute.

It was hard to keep up. "Don't screenshot," he said, before changing the setting to once an hour and the conversation became slightly less rushed.

Weiwei worries about his online trail. Compared with the pre-internet China in which he grew up, the rules have changed. Paper could be destroyed; there is no such safeguard with new media. Telegram has a unique feature that allows users to start a "secret chat" with their contacts. These self-destruct after a chosen interval and supposedly leave no trace.

"It's not that popular yet [in China] and I hope it will stay that way," said Weiwei. Popularity means one thing: the Chinese government will make disabling it a priority. Barely 24 hours after this conversation took place, Telegram was blocked in China – another victim of the country's censorship machine. According to People's Daily (the official newspaper of the Chinese Communist Party), it was singled out for aiding Chinese human-rights lawyers, who have become the target of a recent crackdown.

In June China passed a new national security law. The vagueness of its wording has led many to fear it could be applied widely. It joins a long list of extensions of internet censorship in China this year.

Among the most concerning was the blocking of several prominent virtual private networks (Astrill, Golden Frog and StrongVPN) at the start of 2015. VPNs are easy-to-download systems for anonymously gaining access to the internet via another computer's IP address. Used by millions of Chinese, they have become the main tools for working around the censors – but more recently have been targeted. While some VPNs are still in use, they are reportedly slower and more erratic since the new law, but alternatives are hard to find.

This is the pattern of the free-speech battle in 21st-century China. Sometimes a new product or idea, such as Telegram, enters the market promising to bypass censorship and then it's a matter of time before it's removed or blocked. FreeWeibo, a site which captures all the posts taken off Weibo (China's version of Twitter), is another example among many. →

Smoke and mirrors: how The New York Times skirts Chinese censorship

The New York Times – both the English- and Chinese-language versions – has been blocked in China since October 2012, when an article revealed the private wealth of the then premier, Wen Jiabao. The Times' relationship with China could have ended then – but it didn't.

Not only is it still available in China but its readership is growing. According to Craig Smith, managing director for The New York Times in China, only the US, Canada and the UK represent larger online markets.

"We are indeed regaining our readership and continuing to produce quality journalism in Chinese," Ching-Ching Ni, editor-in-chief of The New York Times' Chinese website, headquartered in Beijing, confirmed to Index.

Ni was not at liberty to reveal more; nor would other Times employees in China when approached by Index. But internet experts who have been watching the company have come to their own conclusions about its success. Many readers are gaining access to the site via VPNs, but The New York Times also uses a variety of measures to make its content accessible to a Chinese audience.

The first is known as mirroring. The NYT distributes new articles across three or four "mirror" sites. These look and feel similar to the original, but are hosted on a different server, making them harder for the censors to track. The alternative server is usually one that is government-sanctioned, and so to block the site officials would have to stymie content they don't otherwise want to block. Amazon's server is often used – to take down that server would affect all the businesses using Amazon in China. Eventually most of these mirror sites are blocked, yet the small window of availability is all the NYT needs to have an impact.

It also uses apps to its advantage. New apps are created, sometimes openly branded with The New York Times name and logo, and articles are distributed on these.

The same goes for social media. While the official account is blocked, unofficial accounts spring up, often under similar names.

Finally, the news organisation also syndicates material to local websites and newspapers, such as QDaily, a popular news aggregator.

None of these measures is foolproof and they all come with potential risks, including fines, prison sentences or, in the case of foreign workers, visa problems. But all is not lost on the wrong side of China's internet censors – so long as one thinks outside the box.

JS

→ Weiwei grew up in the 1980s, a time of perceived freedom after the repressive policies of Mao and before the internet. Has all the new technology brought more or less freedom? "When I was growing up, there were no blogs, no Facebook and the like. The government controlled the media and felt more in control than today," he said. "Now it's harder to stop the flow of information, but it is also spending a lot more money and manpower to censor information than ever before."

The sheer volume of information is the biggest difference from the past. Michel Hockx, director of SOAS China Institute, University of London, writes regularly on Chinese literature and internet culture. He lived in China in the 1980s, when there were fewer newspapers, magazines, books, theatres, concert halls and museums. Everything was more state-controlled and ideological.

"The 1980s was intellectually very free compared to what came before it [the Cultural Revolution], and it was exciting for those doing daring things underground or on university campuses. But the country as a whole and the population as a whole is infinitely freer now than it was in the →

SPECIAL REPORT

CASE STUDY

"I have turned from best-selling author to a creature of the shadows"

Chinese author MURONG XUECUN explains how censorship in the People's Republic is now worse than ever

More than 20,000 words were lost from the China edition of my fourth novel, Dancing Through Red Dust, which is the story of a corrupt Chinese lawyer who ends up on death row. In China, when a publisher tells you your book needs "revisions", they mean "cuts". I could describe corruption, but not the causes of corruption. My corrupt judges could be shown as bad individuals but I was not allowed to criticise the legal system. I could describe life inside China's prisons and remand centres, but had to remove scenes – based on interviews with wardens and former prisoners – that raised controversial issues, such as the system of "cell monitors" (inmates charged with disciplining their cellmates), or the practice of selling organs of death row prisoners.

Seven different publishers read my manuscript before I got a contract. They had described it variously as "a compelling read", "powerful" and "deep" – but none dared offer me a contract. A southern China publisher, after months of hesitation, finally agreed to take it. This is one of the bravest publishers I have known, but unfortunately just months later, they paid a serious price for their courage, because they were forced to shut down. As the publication date approached, the publisher already had serious apprehensions. Several times he told me: "I can't be sure what kind of trouble publishing this book may bring us, so we must prepare and 'do some revisions, a lot of revisions'."

When the Chinese version of the book →

→ 1980s," Professor Hockx told Index. "If you look at what is being published and discussed on the internet nowadays, and you go back to books from the 1980s, you'll see the difference. It's massive."

Certain writers, once banned, are now readily available, said Hockx, mentioning the "Misty Poets" from the 1980s. Their

"Opening a skylight" is a form of protest by which newspapers leave blank space in their printed editions to show where censors removed articles or information

work was often critical of the government but they are now considered giants of the contemporary Chinese literary canon, appearing in every textbook and anthology – showing that criticism of government policy, once a big no-no, is now allowed to a degree. It is the same for translated works: in the 1980s, Lady Chatterley's Lover was banned for being too sexual, but now it can be bought anywhere.

Censorship is no longer "prescriptive" but rather "prohibitive". Hockx explained: "It tells you a few things you cannot say or do, but otherwise anything goes. The majority of people can live with that, so the conflicts are less tense and less significant to most people."

Censorship can still be clunky and obvious, such as when certain films and books are banned. But with a population less willing to put up with restrictions and with more tools to counter them, it tends to be very subtle, especially online.

"In previous years, for instance, Weibo might block an entire sensitive term, such as 'June 4th' or 'Wukan protests'. But now, instead of wholesale blocking, results are more likely to be selectively curated. This gives the appearance of unrestricted access of information but is censorship all the same," said Liz Carter, author of the recently published book Let 100 Voices Speak: How the Internet Is Transforming China and Changing Everything.

As the nature of censorship has shifted, so have counter-censorship measures. They have also become more nuanced and clever. Advanced technologies are used to bypass internet censorship and even simple tools involve an element of craft.

"Getting around content filters does require a lot of creativity, [like] writing words differently, using puns and homonyms and so on," said Carter. "Media outlets, activists and ordinary individuals have found an amazing variety of ways to alert their readers that the government is interfering with the free flow of information."

Hockx said he was struck by how people today, especially China's youth, approached the free-speech battle in a more playful and ironic manner: "The 1980s generation was extremely brave and heroic, and fond of grand gestures. They really gave you the impression that they were fighting the system, but in many ways they were using the same language as the system: the language of revolution, battle, struggle and so on. Nowadays most people just ignore the system or make fun of it, and the language of the system seems strangely outdated and obsolete."

Some of these techniques nevertheless borrow from the past, such as a practice called "opening a skylight". "Opening a skylight is a form of protest by which newspaper editors leave blank space in their printed editions where censors removed articles or information, thereby alerting readers to the censorship," Carter explained. "This was done at least as early as 1911, when one Chinese paper protested the Qing dynasty's censorship of information about the Wuchang Uprising, and it is still occasionally done today."

But the modern form of opening a skylight

SPECIAL REPORT

CASE STUDY CONTINUED...

was released in late 2008, I discovered without any great surprise, that numerous passages on China's legal and justice enforcement systems passages had been "revised" to the extent that there was hardly a trace of them. The censors also demanded a new ending for the book – the original was thought to be unhealthily dark.

The original title of the book was also changed by the publisher, in anticipation of a backlash. I had wanted to use the Chinese characters for *mancheng* (full city) and *yiguan* (officials' hats and robes), loosely translating as A City of Officials. But the Chinese word *yiguan* is often associated with another word, *qinshou*, meaning inhuman. The implication of this title is that the behaviour of the city's impeccably dressed officials is little different from that of beasts. My publisher firmly insisted we change the title to *yuanjing wo* (forgive me) *hong cheng* (red dust, a metaphor for the human world), *diandao* (inverted, confused). *Diandao*, used as a verb, can also articulate a strategy that Chinese writers may adopt by offering inventive explanations of the meaning of words or phrases to make them seem less sensitive. When navigating the censorship process, with all its risks and uncertainties, sometimes our best response is to muddy the waters.

"If censorship cannot be abolished, I hope that it can become more relaxed. If it cannot become more relaxed, I hope it can become more rational," I said in a 2011 talk about censorship. Four years later, I find that more and more books can't be published, more and more topics can't be discussed, more and more authors are being sent to jail for things they said. As for me, I have turned from a best-selling author into a creature of the shadows who often cannot speak out, whose writings cannot be published. China's censorship has not become more relaxed or logical, but ever more strict and stupid. The only positive development is that there are more creatures of the shadows like me now, and we are not frightened like our predecessors were. My friends and I, together with countless other writers, journalists and lawyers, and millions of our fellow citizens, are preparing to welcome a China that enjoys freedom of expression. ⊗

***Murong Xuecun** is an author based in Beijing and Hong Kong. A full English translation of Dancing Through Red Dust, which restores the original ending and other material cut from the Chinese edition, is published by Make-Do Publishing and comes out this month*

will see outlets alerting the reader to censorship through allusions or catchphrases. For example, during a press conference at the start of China's annual parliamentary session in early 2014, a government representative responded to journalists' questions on the highly sensitive trial of former state security chief Zhou Yongkang with the words "you understand". The implication was he could only reveal so much. Since then, Chinese media have used the phrase "you understand" to signify the unsayable.

Free-speech advocates are nervous about Xi Jinping's China and rightly so. This summer alone has seen the arrest of scores of human-rights lawyers, as well as the new national-security legislation. Fewer topics are out of bounds, but those which are remain fiercely guarded. Despite this, the situation has improved from the recent past, and when censorship does take place there are ways around it – if only for a fleeting moment. ⊗

***Jemimah Steinfeld** is a contributing editor to Index on Censorship magazine. She is a former contributor to CNN China and Time Out China. Her book Little Emperors and Material Girls: Sex and Youth in Modern China is out now*

a specific location, that person ha
uld go on until the material reache
various ways. I was often given a
paper with a message. I would be told
an whom I would recognise only by a specific
lipstick and then she would keep it in her purse
ontents of the tube: we simply received it an
chocolates or even chewing gum
lowing us, so we developed a wa
Miguel and I were on our wa
e, a tall man gave
nd out about it and we
n exchange a
evabee

Smugglers' tales

44(03): 14/17 | DOI: 10.1177/0306422015605695

How do you move forbidden information in and out of authoritarian states? **Index** reports three stories, past and present, featuring brave and inventive techniques: hiding notes in lipstick containers in post-coup Chile, swapping a bag of bananas for documents in communist Czechoslovakia, and concealing flash drives in cigarette boxes to sneak films and music into North Korea

CHILE

Lip service

NANCY MARTÍNEZ-VILLARREAL recounts how she smuggled information in lipstick around 1970s' Chile to evade Pinochet's surveillance

I joined the Revolutionary Left Movement (MIR) in Chile around 1971 or 1972. Some wholesalers had hidden food supplies in warehouses to destabilise Salvador Allende's Popular Unity government, so the stores were empty and people weren't even able to buy the most basic goods. I didn't want to stay home doing nothing while others suffered, so I joined a cell of the MIR as a messenger.

After the 1973 coup d'état, which brought to power the army commander-in-chief, General Augusto Pinochet, many dear friends were killed or tortured by the secret police. But my cell remained active.

Our mission was to provide information to the highest ranks of the MIR. Each of us had to deliver pieces of information to someone in a specific location, that person had to hand the content to another comrade, and so it would go on until the material reached the party leaders.

The information was smuggled in various ways. I was often given a lipstick tube containing a small piece of handwritten paper with a message. I would be told to go into the toilet of a hospital and meet a woman whom I would recognise only by a specific code. She would simply ask to borrow my lipstick and then she would keep it in her purse. We weren't allowed to open or read the contents of the tube: we simply received it and transported it. On other occasions we used flour packages, chocolates or even chewing gum.

Pinochet's secret police were always following us, so we developed a way to alert each other in case of danger. Once my boyfriend, Miguel, and I were on our way to hand someone a lipstick tube in a public square. Before we got there, a tall man gave me a look that implied we had to abort the operation. The police had found out about it and we risked being arrested. It's difficult to describe it now, but we didn't even exchange a word. His look told me everything.

Months later, there was a big police operation and many were arrested, among them a very good friend of mine. She found a way to send me a message, telling me to stay home and do nothing. She ended up being taken to a torture centre and exiled to Europe.

I carried on sporadically collaborating with the MIR, but then I married Miguel and had children, so I decided to bring them up in a safe environment. My husband continued his struggle against Pinochet, although by other means, including joining a civil organisation that aimed to teach and prepare people for the 1988 referendum, in which a majority rejected an extension of Pinochet's rule.

Like many others, I'm just an anonymous Chilean who wanted to contribute her grain of sand to a worthy cause. In those years, I had the chance to meet many people who are now in power, but they seem to have forgotten about all that.

I am really proud of what I did and I would happily do it all over again. The dictatorship was horrible and many people died, but we did manage to save a few lives as well. And that makes everything worthwhile.

Nancy Martínez-Villarreal *is a retired primary-school teacher who lives in Santiago. Translated by César Jiménez-Martínez*

Smoke signals

The North Korean defector KIM JOON YOUNG* explains how information is smuggled into North Korea using cigarette packets, car tyres and flash drives

On the border between North Korea and China, along the Tumen and Yalu rivers, thousands of North Korean soldiers keep watch. In one of the most isolated and repressive countries in the world, the military's job is two-fold: stop people getting out; stop information getting in. When you look from the Chinese side, it is difficult to see the guards, but they are there, hiding in strategic holes dug in the ground, sitting quietly and observing.

Every so often the soldiers spot something suspicious floating in the river. One of the ways people smuggle foreign content into North Korea is to put it on a flash drive and hide it in cigarette boxes. You carefully wrap the boxes with plastic bags and tie them to a spare tyre. Parts of the river are only a few metres wide and there you can throw the tyre into the water. The soldiers will see you; later, when nobody is looking at them, they will pick up the tyre, take the cigarettes and find the flash drive inside.

These soldiers are typically young and curious. Being on watch can become lonely and solitary. They are tempted by this China contraband, including flash drives and DVDs with South Korean programmes and foreign movies, all of which are strictly forbidden. The flash drives carry content that is fresh and different from everything that North Koreans know.

The soldiers might watch the content on their computers or portable DVD players, or sell it on the black market. Perhaps they will report it, but then their supervisors will end up watching the content anyway. It will be quickly passed on among family and close friends, and it is through this curiosity that North Koreans are slowly beginning to understand the outside world, personal freedoms and opportunities for choice. This is why the national leader, Kim Jong-un, has recently tried to cut down on banned music through house-to-house searches.

What threatens this authoritarian regime most is external information getting into the ears, minds and, eventually, mouths of its controlled citizens.

Kim Joon Young *is a pseudonym for a representative of the North Korea Strategy Center, a Seoul-based NGO*

CZECHOSLOVAKIA

Forbidden fruit

ROBERT MCCRUM on how he exchanged bananas for documents in the former Czechoslovakia

Once upon a time, almost impossible to recall today, the East-West border snaking through Mitteleuropa, from Szczecin in the Baltic to Trieste on the Adriatic, exercised quite a spell. It was a place of jeopardy, historical consequence and icy superpower confrontation.

Frontiers are always cool, and the Iron Curtain was super-cool. The watchtowers, arc lights and frozen-faced guards policing a divided Europe had a tangible noir chic.

Looking back, I confess to the thrill of crossing to the dark side, especially going by train, particularly at night. I did this several times from the ages of 17 (heading for Moscow via the German Democratic Republic), to 30-something (from Vienna to Warsaw).

On one occasion, in the 1980s, I also smuggled literary contraband into Czechoslovakia (as it was then), returning to the West with precious dissident material hidden in my suitcase. Which is how I came to be on the Berlin-Prague express with some banned copies of Index on Censorship – and a bag of bananas – in the spring of 1982.

Three coincidences had conspired to arouse my interest in Czechoslovakia and to propel me inexorably eastwards. First, in 1981, I had received a letter from a Prague bookseller named Peter Cisar, asking for a signed copy of a novel I'd written. A minor correspondence ensued and I flirted unsuccessfully with the idea of a meeting. (Later, I would use the experience in The Fabulous Englishman, another novel – but that's another story.)

At about this time, I had also joined the board of Index, then under the editorship of George Theiner. George was a gentle, modest, expatriate Czech, with whom I became friends, and his memories of his home town were another prompt for my journey. Finally, as an editor for Faber & Faber, I was given the extraordinary opportunity to publish Milan Kundera's most recent novel, The Book of Laughter and Forgetting. That's certainly another story.

But in the end, I went simply as a kind of clandestine courier. The bananas were a ruse – a mixture of pretext and decoy.

In those distant days, fruit and vegetables were so scarce in the Eastern Bloc that Western visitors were encouraged to take fresh fruit as gifts for their hosts. Theiner also advised that a supermarket bag of, say, bananas would be sufficiently frivolous to distract any inquisitive border guard.

Passing through the Iron Curtain was never a trivial matter. Some years before my trip to Prague, I saw a fellow passenger bundled off the Moscow train at Brest-Litovsk. I will never forget the look on his face as he was dragged past our carriage.

So with my bag of half-ripe bananas I duly arrived at the main station in Prague – where I was met by a young Misha Glenny, just starting out on his career as a distinguished foreign correspondent. I was introduced to several key figures in the Czech literary underground, handed over my copies of Index on Censorship and received various documents to bring back to the West.

Without the bananas, my return journey was edgier, but I got through. The next time I saw the Iron Curtain, it was October 1991. The checkpoints were deserted, and a strange episode in European history was over. ⊗

***Robert McCrum** is an associate editor of The Observer newspaper*

SEARCH STRIP
by Martin Rowson
1
REMIND ME, WHAT'S WITH THIS CAT THING AGAIN?
HOW MANY TIMES DO I HAVE TO EXPLAIN THIS? LOOK...
2
YOU ARE AWARE OF THE CENTRAL COMMITTEE'S LATEST CRACKDOWN ON DISSIDENT BLOGS, AREN'T YOU?
OF COURSE!
3
AND YOU DO REMEMBER HOW THE FULL APPARATUS OF STATE SECURITY IS NOW MONITORING ALL INTERNET TRAFFIC WITH EVEN GREATER DILIGENCE THAN EVER, YES?
NATURALLY!
4
AND SURELY YOU HAVEN'T FORGOTTEN THAT 6 MONTHS YOU & I SPENT IN A LABOUR CAMP FOR "CRIMINAL HOOLIGANISM"?
HOW COULD I?

MARTIN ROWSON: Martin is the regular cartoonist for Index on Censorship. He is also the author of graphic novels including Gulliver's Travels and The Life and Opinions of Tristram Shandy, Gentelman,

From murder to bureaucratic mayhem

44(03): 20/22 | DOI: 10.1177/0306422015605706

Argentina's press freedom has come a long way since its junta sought to silence criticism by killing journalists. But is it free of censorship? **Andrew Graham-Yooll** assesses what happened after the regime crumbled, and looks at the new means of controlling the message

LEFT: Relatives of the people "disappeared" during the Argentinean dictatorship carry images of their loved ones through central Buenos Aires in 2008

WHAT DOES NOT change over the decades is the desire of those in power to limit information which might be unsuitable to their needs. Why should Argentina be different?

Nearly four decades ago the military regime (1976-83) of General Jorge Rafael Videla went from threatening and terrorising journalists, as a means of controlling information, to murdering them. More than 100 journalists were killed during the seven-year rule of the armed forces, but that figure was hardly reported in the establishment press. The absence of that record often turned on the argument that the dead were "not real" journalists; that they were not newsroom hacks, but militants of different political organisations. The public lived in a state of denial, so the crimes were ignored: those killed "must have done something".

Freedom of expression has moved on a bit. They don't kill journalists any more. Harassment is more common. For journalists of a certain age who worked through the 1970s, there has never been so much freedom to criticise a government as now. One magazine (Noticias) even printed an artist's impression of a woman, with a close resemblance to the president, in full orgasm. In return, the aides of President Cristina Fernández de Kirchner have used contrived "show trials", held on a stage in front of Government House, to "try" well-known media personalities accused of siding with the military during the dictatorship. The government also publicly insulted opposition scribes and commentators. In April 2008, the president lashed out at Clarín's political cartoonist, Hermenegildo Sabat, for a drawing that showed Fernández with her lips closed with an X. She accused him of a "mafia-style warning".

The election of Raúl Alfonsín as president in 1983 marked the end of military rule and the beginning of a new democratic age. Film production flourished; Luis Puenzo won an Oscar for his 1985 film, The Official Story, which told of babies borne by captives who were murdered. Radio became more daring and, while government-run television had limitations, newspapers could claim never to have supported the military. Fear had not vanished, but it was good to see the alternative press trying to find test their limits.

The 1990s saw a free-for-all. Carlos Saúl Menem became president in 1989 and was re-elected in 1995. He sold state television to friendly media owners and bought goodwill with generous arrangements, just as he made profitable associations with editors, columnists, trade unionists, police and members of the judiciary. In the mid-90s the rot set in, with rampant corruption and gross abuse of power. This included destruction of evidence of illegal arms sales to Ecuador and Croatia between 1991 and 1995: a munitions factory in Córdoba province was blown up, leaving seven dead, 300 injured and a town devastated. Reputable columnists in the press were seen as more reliable than the courts and people resorted to them, to mediate in conflicts and court cases.

The lobbies hit back. In the summer of 1997, a 35-year-old photographer, José Luis Cabezas, was murdered, allegedly at the instigation of a business tycoon, Alfredo Yabrán, who had forbidden the press to photograph him and who was close to the Menem administration. Nine men were charged and sentenced for the murder; Yabrán committed suicide in 1998. It was the high-point of confrontation between the press and government.

In 1999, Menem left office with the country in crisis. Argentina faced financial disaster in December 2001. There were riots and looting. Menem's successor, Fernando de la Rúa, resigned and Argentina had five presidents in a week. In January 2002, a former Menem associate, Eduardo Duhalde, was elected by the national assembly to complete the presidential term to 2005. But Duhalde called elections and handed over government to Néstor Kirchner in 2003.

Kirchner promised change. He even →

Credit: DigitalVues / Alamy

→ won praise from freedom-of-expression NGO Article 19 for sending Congress a bill freeing access to information. It has never been passed.

Nearly 40 years on from military dictatorship, Argentina's line in the limitations on freedom of expression has changed. It's hard to say when to yell "censor" and when it would be a false alarm. Cristina Fernández de Kirchner succeeded her husband in 2007. Néstor died suddenly in 2010. She continued the policy he had set: do not censor, gain full control of the media.

Freedom of expression has moved on. They don't kill journalists any more. Harassment is more common

The three main newspapers in Buenos Aires – Clarín, La Nación and Perfil – are critical of the government. Allegations of repression range from failure to provide state advertising to frequent insults by officials. Argentina's Newspaper Publishers Association (ADEPA) clocked up nine serious protests over attacks on journalists and publications between 12 September 2014 and 8 April 2015 (and four more protests more recently). The Association for Civil Rights (ADC) has been active in questioning the constitutionality of government intentions (such as a plan to restrict some internet contents).

But is this censorship? The protests and demands are published widely, which is evidence of freedom of expression. What has replaced censorship is the massive control of the media by the government through favoured supporters becoming its owners. The government encouraged business allies and supporters to buy into existing companies, facilitating the purchases with generous credits and assuring proprietors abundant and well-paid government advertising.

Some government opponents describe the new media law, a reform needed for more than half a century, as a weapon for censorship. But the law of audiovisual communications services, passed in October 2009, has been bogged down in court actions which question its validity and effects. It includes six clauses, tamely voted for by Fernández's majority in Congress, aimed almost specifically at facilitating the takeover or break-up of the Clarín Group – one of Latin America's largest media companies. The Kirchners saw Clarín as their real political "enemy" and sought to destroy it. The clauses in question have reached the Supreme Court, which has rejected them in part. The six-year-old battle continues.

Fernández's regime, which constitutionally comes to an end on 10 December this year, has used its allies to gain influence at more than 100 newspapers, television channels and radio stations up and down the country. The most recent purchase was made by a construction tycoon and controller of gambling venues, Cristobal López, who bought the financial paper Ambito Financiero, including purchase of the 139-year-old, English-language daily Buenos Aires Herald. And by acquiring media influence, Fernández has also put pressure on the courts, on business, on just about everything. Now she has to go, her ambition only partly reached.

So Argentina has gone from murder to bureaucratic mayhem, with only some of the media and the courts able to keep a check on government. The country lives without full freedom of expression, but the means of pressure have changed. Fernandéz has to step down in December, but she is clinging to the influence she has built up in government with a view to a comeback – and a new catalogue of excesses against Argentina's critical media. ⊗

Andrew Graham-Yooll *OBE was editor of Index between 1989 and 1993. He was the editor of the Buenos Aires Herald from 1994 to 2007. He lives in Buenos Aires*

Words of warning

44(03): 24/27 | DOI: 10.1177/0306422015605707

As pressure on the South African media grows, **Raymond Joseph**, who was a young reporter during apartheid, compares then with now

Credit: Ian Berry/Magnum

ABOVE: Nelson Mandela at an ANC rally in 1994. In the same year, Mandela addressed the International Press Institute Congress in Cape Town and said: "A critical, independent and investigative press is the lifeblood of any democracy"

WHEN A STATE of emergency was declared in South Africa in 1986, many newspapers carried warnings on their front pages. Each was worded slightly differently, but the message was essentially the same: because of the state of emergency, what you are reading in this newspaper may not necessarily reflect all sides of the story.

It was a dangerous time for journalists whose media organisations opposed the apartheid regime. Harvey Tyson, a former editor of The Star, suggested that it was a bit like trying to navigate a minefield wearing a blindfold. He was referring to a glut of restrictive laws made even tougher during the state of emergency.

For instance, there was a clause in the Police Act that made it an offence to publish "untrue" information about police or police operations. Lawyers warned that journalists and their editors could be prosecuted for publishing "untrue" information and, →

The Foreign Press Association in London
11 Carlton House Terrace SW1Y 5AJ Telephone: 01-930 0445
PRESS 1985
PRESS 1985
PRESS 1985
Name RAYMOND JOSEPH
Organisation SOUTH AFRICAN MORNING NEWSPAPERS
Signature of Holder:
Handtekening van Houer:
1994/ № 0310
Press Card
This is to certify that :
MR RAYMOND JOSEPH
is a :
JOURNALIST
Signature of holder:
97-1128
10/97
PRESS CARD — PERSKAART
This is to certify that the holder of this card
Hiermee word gesertifiseer dat die houer van hierdie
kaart
RAY JOSEPH
is a staff member of
is 'n stafid van
SUNDAY TIMES
of
van
Johannesburg
Commissioner of the South African Police.
Uitgereik deur die PERSUNIE VAN SUID-AFRIKA
kragtens sy Ooreenkoms met die Kommissaris
van die Suid-Afrikaanse Polisie.
Signature of Holder
Handtekening van Houer
Date
Datum
7/1/82
Editor/Redakteur
Commissioner: S.A. Police
Kommissaris: S.A. Polisie
A № 443

ABOVE: Press photos from Ray Joseph's decades as a journalist in South Africa

→ as a safeguard, needed to seek police comment before publication. But police inevitably dismissed most stories as untrue, leading to a Catch-22 situation. Stories were often spiked, or only ran after major surgery with crucial facts omitted.

Mandela told the gathering: "A critical, independent and investigative press is the lifeblood of any democracy"

One experience, just a few days after the Soweto uprisings of June 1976, is telling. I climbed a tree to peer over the walls of the fortress-like police station in the black township of Alexandra, Johannesburg. To my horror, I saw at least a dozen bodies – people who had died in clashes with police that day, laid out in a courtyard. My newspaper's lawyers said I had to take the information to the police, who denied what I had seen. My story never ran and the official toll declared by police for that brutal and bloody day was far lower than the number of dead I saw with my own eyes.

When the African National Congress swept to power in 1994, many of us hoped this heralded a new era in government and media relations. Our optimism grew after an address to the International Press Institute Congress in Cape Town in 1994 by the ANC leader, Nelson Mandela, who a few months later would become president of the new, democratic South Africa.

Mandela told the gathering: "A critical, independent and investigative press is the

Credit: Ray Joseph

lifeblood of any democracy. The press must be free from state interference ... It is only such a free press that can have the capacity to relentlessly expose excesses and corruption on the part of the government, state officials and other institutions that hold power in society."

But under the current president, Jacob Zuma, the relationship between the media and the governing ANC is steadily worsening. The party persistently pursues the idea of a media-appeals tribunal, deriving from a resolution at its 2007 national conference in Polokwane. This gained further traction when a 2010 ANC discussion document argued that freedom of the press was not an absolute right and needed to be "balanced against individual rights to privacy and human dignity".

Legal experts have warned that such a tribunal may not pass constitutional muster, but the ANC wields it as a sword of Damocles. Even sweeping changes to the Press Council have not assuaged party leaders' periodic rants against the media.

In July the ANC treasurer general, Zweli Mkhize, said that, while his party believed in a free press, South Africa's media were far too critical. The ANC often felt that criticism from the media was "unwarranted" and "unfair", he told the annual general meeting of the SA National Editors Forum. He highlighted among other things the reporting of the secret departure from South Africa of the Sudanese president, Omar Al Bashir, in defiance of a court order banning him from leaving the country until an application calling for his arrest had been heard. He is wanted by the International Criminal Court for alleged war crimes and crimes against humanity.

Just a day later it was reported that the "triple alliance" – the old anti-apartheid bloc of the ANC, the trade-union federation COSATU and the South African Communist Party – would renew the push for a media tribunal. "It cannot be that everybody is subject to independent checks and balances and then you have a section of the society which is so influential ... but only intends to do self-regulation," said Blade Nzimande, secretary-general of the SACP.

These attacks are not unrelated to the reporting of government corruption and in particular the scandal of more than ZAR250 million (over $20 million) of taxpayers' money being spent on President Zuma's private estate in Nkandla.

Amber lights are flashing as the press gears itself up to see off any new attempts to restrict its hard-won freedoms

Despite all this, South Africa still has one of the freest presses on the continent, with no real restrictions on reporting, often robust and fearless, and investigative reporting enjoying a golden age. But amber lights are flashing as the press gears itself up once again to see off any new attempts to restrict its hard-won freedoms – which could take it back to the dark days when journalists had to constantly look over their shoulders and be careful of what they reported.

***Raymond Joseph** has worked as a journalist in South Africa since 1973. He is based in Cape Town and is a Knight/ICFJ international journalism fellow. He tweets @rayjoe*

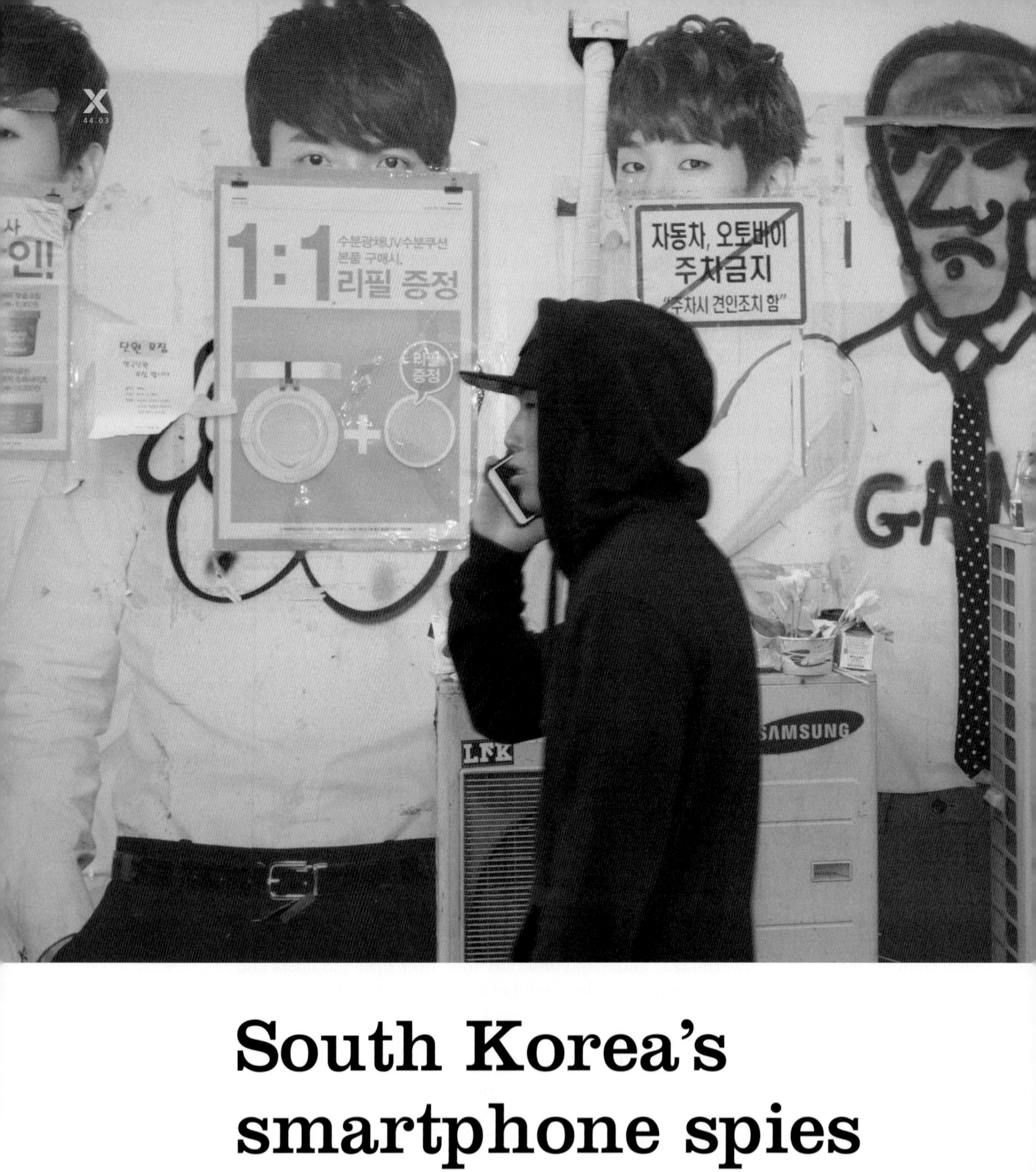

Credit: Bruno Barbey/Magnum Photos

South Korea's smartphone spies

44(03): 28/31 | DOI: 10.1177/0306422015605708

A new South Korean law embeds a surveillance tool on teenagers' phones – just another example of the country's paternalistic attitudes, reports **Steven Borowiec**

LEFT: South Korean teenagers are online, connected and many have smart phones. A newly amended law requires all telephone companies to install censorship software in all smartphones sold to users under 19

ATTEMPTS TO VISIT many South Korean websites bring the user to the same screen, an artless white and blue image with a warning announcing that the Korea Communications Standards Commission, the national censor, has placed this site off limits. The sites behind this digital roadblock could contain pornography, or materials from North Korea or information about Islamic extremism.

This is the current frontline in the South Korean state's efforts to keep its citizens from content which censors deem objectionable, embodying a paternalism that goes back at least to Korea's time as a Japanese colony (1910-45). Japan instituted comprehensive censorship, which particularly affected journalists, writers, filmmakers and artists. South Korea's first post-independence rulers kept these practices largely in place, and the legacy remains.

In April, the Enforcement Decree of the amended Telecommunications Business Act came into effect. The decree requires all South Korean telecommunications companies to install censorship software in all smartphones sold to users under 19. The government provides the app for free, purportedly to block minors from accessing any "harmful" materials – it gets to decide what constitutes "harmful".

Korean and foreign-language websites that publish overtly violent or sexual material are blocked, as well as sites associated with North Korea or terrorist groups. Some South Koreans use apps, which conceal their IP address, to gain access to blocked websites, but censors tend to catch up and block those, too. Finding and installing these apps is, in any event, beyond the technical know-how of many young people.

In 2015, most censorship takes place online: South Korea has the highest broadband internet penetration in the world. The KCSC employs an army of energetic censors across a number of bureaux, each assigned a different branch of the media or cyberspace, to manage what its people can view – always a moving target.

The South Korean government's goal has not just been to maintain law and order, but to encourage certain norms and ethics in the populace. "That's the government's job, to maintain a nice, clean internet," an unnamed KCSC official told Wired in 2009.

"In the pre-modern period, the government's objective was mainly to produce virtuous subjects; nowadays it means economically productive people who will go through school, get jobs, marry and produce children," said Se-woong Koo, a lecturer at Yonsei University who has written for →

→ The New York Times about censorship in South Korea.

Shortly after Korean independence, discord broke out between the south and the north and their allies. Censorship south of the 38th parallel initially focused on preventing the spread of information related to North Korea. Hence the National Security Law of 1948. Its stated objective is "to suppress anti-state acts that endanger national security and to ensure nation's security, people's life and freedom" – specifically, to prevent North Korean cells from operating in the south.

Even after the fighting ended in 1953, South Korean governments kept the National Security Law on the books, with critics accusing them of using it to stifle free speech. Indeed cases taken under it have increased in recent years. In May Human Rights Watch called the law a "Cold War relic that criminalizes criticism", recommending its repeal or revision.

The peak period of censorship was under Park Chung-hee, president from 1961 to 1979, when there were clearer rules as to what kind of cultural content was permitted. Park passed laws that prohibited criticism of his regime, most notably Emergency Ordinance #1, which mandated jail time for government critics. Under him, women were forbidden from wearing miniskirts in public, and police were known to make sure men's hair didn't exceed a certain length (the prohibition on miniskirts ended only in 2006 and although long hair for men is now legal it is not common).

The heavy-handed tactics continued through the military regimes of the early- and mid- 1980s, but the democratisation movement later that decade issued in major civic and political changes. Before hosting the 1988 Summer Olympics, the Chun Doo-hwan government relaxed restrictions on the press and agreed to multi-party elections. That was the beginning of a free press

Are the kids are all right?

In Seoul's late afternoon, the streets fill with gaggles of high-school students. Out in the brief break between classes and dinner at home, they walk in groups, many half stuck to their smartphones.

Controlling what young people can and cannot gain access to is a priority for South Korean censors: 99.6 per cent of teenagers are online and many have smartphones.

Yet on a recent afternoon in Seoul's busy Dongdaemun area, none of more than a dozen students queried had ever heard of the decree (see main story). None was aware that their smartphones contained censorship software. When told what kinds of content were blocked by the app, one 16-year-old girl called Park giggled sheepishly: "I wouldn't go looking for any of that anyway."

While some activists have decried the decree as an invasion of young people's privacy, and some parents have called it an intrusion on their rights as parents, there hasn't been much organised resistance. South Korean adults work extremely long hours, compared with other developed countries, and so don't have much time to look over their kids' shoulders.

Most therefore don't object to government help in keeping young people on the straight and narrow. "Many parents view the government as some sort of omniscient or all-powerful being that should take care of problems, even if that means parents giving away their liberties," said Park Kyungsin, Open Net's director.

SB

in South Korea, and today its media operate free of censorship.

The development of the internet brought censors new concerns, with South Koreans now having access to all kinds of content and the means to post their own criticisms. A 2005 law required all users to use their real names when posting anything online. Its official aim was to prevent the spread of false information online, but critics alleged it was really intended to make users fearful of posting anything that might upset the censors.

This rationale had ample legal precedent in South Korea. "Legislative invocation of a concern for public morals is usually a politically popular justification for government regulation," wrote Jaewan Moon in a 2003 article in the Washington University Global Studies Law Review. When the law was scrapped in 2012, the Constitutional Court found no evidence that it had stopped the dissemination of false information – only that it had undermined free speech.

After 10 years of liberal rule, in 2008 South Korean politics took a turn to the right with the election of a conservative government, succeeded in 2013 by the administration of Park Geun-hye, daughter of Park Chung-hee. President Park and much of her cabinet are cut from the same cloth as her father, prioritising political and economic security over civil liberties.

The government has stepped up efforts to police cyberspace. In the best known example of this encroachment, the national spy agency was found to have used agents to post comments on online message boards voicing support for Park Geun-hye when she was running for president in 2012. Park Kyungsin, one of South Korea's most dogged anti-censorship activists and director of Open Net, an NGO which presses for internet freedom in South Korea, estimates that each year 500,000 websites are taken down – though he says this covers only South Korea's three main portals and that the total is probably much higher.

Seoul continues to invest in the internet as a way of driving economic growth, but nevertheless remains uncomfortable with the freedom the web allows its citizens. "The government puts a lot of effort into building its internet infrastructure, but it doesn't have a lot of trust in its people to use the internet on their own," said Geoffrey Cain, South Korea researcher for the Open Government Partnership.

The government provides the app for free, purportedly to block minors from accessing any "harmful" materials – it gets to decide what constitutes "harmful"

There is far less censorship in South Korea than under the military governments of the 1970s and 80s. Due to the popular movements of the 1980s, the media operate without government control, and the country's buzzing online sphere provides a forum for free expression. But the current government, staffed with many senior officials who worked in the harsh regimes of decades past, is always looking for ways to use that tool of free expression – the internet – to spy on its critics.

***Steven Borowiec** is a journalist and regular contributor to Index on Censorship magazine. He is based in South Koreaß*

“We lost journalism in Russia”

44(03): 32/35 | DOI: 10.1177/0306422015605709

Andrei Aliaksandrau examines the evolution of censorship in Russia, from Soviet institutions to today’s blend of influence and pressure

LEFT: Journalists from independent Russian media start-up Meduza meet in their newsroom. Meduza has been publishing from Riga, Latvia, since October 2014

Credit: Ints Kalnins/ Reuters

"IT WAS STRAIGHTFORWARD censorship. Editorial couriers brought copies of all newspaper pages to Glavlit offices before publishing. If an article had to do with army, a stamp of military censor was also necessary," recollected Aliaksandr Klaskouski, now the head of analytical projects at BelaPAN Information Company in Belarus.

The General Directorate for the Protection of State Secrets in the Press (Glavlit) was the institution of direct state censorship in the Soviet Union. This body was attached to the Council of Ministers of the USSR, and was responsible for the pre-censoring of all books, magazines and movies. No piece of literature or journalism could be published without its authorisation. Its aim was to "fight anti-Soviet propaganda" and provide the population with the right – the one and only – point of view on events.

Direct censorship is now forbidden by the constitutions of post-Soviet countries – but censorship still exists, in different forms.

Journalists at Meduza, one of the most popular Russian-language online news websites, now based in Riga, Latvia, managed to find only two instances when censorship was officially admitted in modern Russia. In 2006 an official in the Altay region was sentenced to a suspended term of 10 months in prison for making the local press write only positive things about the governor and forbidding critical publications. Six years later, a court overruled a decision by the head of a local administration in the same region, which had created a special commission to check articles in local newspapers before publication.

No other cases of direct official censorship have been noted – yet still Russia is regarded as having one of the worst press freedom environments in the world (180th place out of 199 countries in Freedom House's Freedom of the Press 2015 ranking).

The most brutal way journalists are silenced in Russia is physical violence and assassinations. According to Reporters Without Borders, 27 journalists have been killed in Russia since 2002. Impunity is still a huge issue. The most famous cases, like the murders of Anna Politkovskaya in 2006, Natalya Estemirova in 2009 or Akhmednabi Akhmednabiyev in 2013, were never truly investigated; the instigators of their murders were never found.

The state finds other ways to control what is being said on the main TV channels.

"Television has been under total control of the state for quite a while. All major channels belong to the state," said Pavel →

→ Sheremet, an award-winning TV journalist with experience of work in Belarus, Russia and Ukraine. "Fifteen years ago editors-in-chief of main TV channels were invited for weekly meeting to Kremlin to discuss the most important topics and events. Now all newsrooms work under constant direct supervision from Kremlin. All big media holdings either belong to the state or to oligarchs from Putin's close circle. So, it is easy for the authorities to control their editorial policies and make them say whatever they need to be transmitted to the society."

"The topics for television are being dictated directly," confirmed Andrei Soldatov, editor of the Agentura.ru website. "This diktat is more indirect in radio, newspapers and online media, where an opinion on how to cover events is being transmitted through editors and owners. As a result we face the most awful kind of censorship – self-censorship, when journalists try to guess how to do a story and put [emphasis] in a way to please his or her editor and owner."

All big media holdings either belong to the state or to oligarchs from Putin's close circle

The new media environment, with the increasing importance of internet and social networks, has given rise to new modes of censorship. The past year saw the introduction of a series of restrictive laws controlling the flow of information online in Russia. For instance, a law tackling "harmful information" on the internet makes it possible to block websites without a court decision, if the authorities find its content to be "potentially harmful for children". Other laws ban "propaganda of homosexuality" or "extremist information" – with definitions and provisions set so broadly and in general terms that they easily allow arbitrary usage.

But some people say censorship in Russia is not about legal restrictions or pressure on journalists. Irada Guseynova, an independent media expert, does not believe the level of censorship in today's Russia is significant.

"If you pop into a bookshop in Moscow, you will find books about Khodorkovsky, one of the main critics of Putin, or other publications that can be seen as critical to the authorities. You can still watch Dozhd TV, or listen to radio station Echo of Moscow, or read Novaya Gazeta. The most awful problem is that we lost journalism in Russia almost entirely. The society does not want true journalism – and journalists easily gave in. You know, in 1954 a famous Soviet writer

CASE STUDY

The way you spin it

HELEN WOMACK on the past 20 years reporting from Russia, from a cautious welcome to be declared a Russophobe

Soviet citizens were cautious but keen to meet me when I first went to Moscow in 1985. They adopted false names and scrambled their telephone numbers when they gave me their contact details, lest my maid, who we assumed worked for the KGB, go through my address book.

Gorbachev was in power but glasnost (openness) was yet to be introduced. There was censorship and propaganda, and my Soviet friends took the news with a heavy pinch of salt. They were hungry for information from the West.

I particularly remember one evening, when they showed me a *samizdat* (self-published) copy of George Orwell's 1984. It wasn't even typed but written out by hand in a school exercise book. The "publisher", who risked jail for his work, had illustrated the dystopian novel with maps of Eastasia, Eurasia and Oceania.

Readers could borrow the book for one night before they were expected to pass it on.

Now my Russian friends, some of whom have stayed with me since that time, still love me – but Russians in general are less excited to meet me. There is no censorship – you can find any information, although you may have to search the net for it – but there is heavy propaganda, which the population seems to swallow uncritically. And fewer people read books.

It is hard to say what changes are global and generational and what are down to the policies of President Vladimir Putin. Recently an extremist Russian website declared me a "pathological Russophobe". In a move that may or may not be connected and political, the Russian Foreign Ministry has found fault with my paperwork and I am no longer able to operate in Moscow as a freelance journalist.

After the love affair comes disillusion. I date Russians' resentment towards the West to the 1999 Nato bombing of Belgrade, but it has got much worse since the row over Crimea and the war in Ukraine. Recently, two Russian journalists were taken hostage in eastern Ukraine. Pro-Kremlin LifeNews rang me up and asked if I would speak in a televised panel discussion "in defence of my colleagues". I agreed, and expressed my concern for the two Russians, while pointing out that Ukrainian journalists and OSCE observers had also been taken hostage.

But I was outgunned on the programme by a barrage of pro-Kremlin voices and realised I had been used as a "useful idiot" to give the show a semblance of balance. I started to question whether I could call such propagandists my colleagues.

Western publications also fail to meet the standards of balance in which I was trained and still believe. I wrote a nuanced piece for The Times, describing belligerent attitudes in Moscow but doubting that Russians seriously want war with the West, only to find the headline writers have come up with: "Russia's young and poor crave war with the West".

It's all in the way you spin it. My heart sinks. Perhaps it is a good thing that I am now out of Russia, in exile in Budapest. I love Russia too much to be part of this ugly information war. ⊗

Helen Womack *reported from Moscow from 1985-2015. She is the author of The Ice Walk: Surviving the Soviet Break-up and the New Russia (Melrose Books, 2013)*

Mikhail Sholokhov said: 'Our enemies from abroad blame us for writing on orders from the communist party. But the thing is that each of us write on orders of our heart – and our hearts belong to the party'. I guess this is the problem – journalists' hearts nowadays still 'belong to the party'. If we do not have a market for quality critical journalism, and do not have people who could teach young journalists to think critically and report professionally, the only way is to 'sell their hearts to the party', to listen to what that 'party' tells you is right – and finally to start believing it is the only correct opinion and go on reporting according to that opinion. In such a situation you do not really have to censor such reporting. We lost journalism in Russia. We have propaganda and campaigning instead." ⊗

Andrei Aliaksandrau *is a journalist based in Belarus*

evabee

Indian films on the cutting-room floor

44(03): 36/39 | DOI: 10.1177/0306422015605711

India's film censors are only too happy to stop films they don't like reaching audiences. Not much has changed since the 1950s, argues **Suhrith Parthasarathy**, after interviewing a censored director

DIRECTOR KUPPUSAMY GANESAN'S fight with India's censors has only just begun. In May this year, the Central Board of Film Certification announced that it had refused to certify Porkalathil Oru Poo, a Tamil-language film, directed by Ganesan. Allowing the film's screening, the film board said, could potentially strain "friendly relations with foreign states", in this case, India's with Sri Lanka. Ganesan has appealed the board's decision to the appellate forum, and he plans to fight the case all the way to the Supreme Court of India, if necessary. "I hope there's some sort of resolution to the issue in the next few months," Ganesan told Index. "If I'm not successful before the censorship authorities, I'll fight the case in the courts, and I hope I can screen the film by October or so."

Porkalathil Oru Poo portrays the life of Isaipriya, a Tamil journalist, who, according to footage first released by the British TV station Channel 4, was killed by the Sri Lankan army during the final days of the civil war that ravaged the country. According to Sattanathapuram Venkataraman Shekhar, one of the members of the board, Ganesan was unable to provide any evidence to the authorities on Isaipriya's actual fate. "Apart from the fact that this could affect our relationship with Sri Lanka," Shekar told Index, "the film also shows India in a bad light. The film seems to suggest that India didn't help out during the civil war. How can we show this to the Indian public?"

The CBFC derives its authority from India's Cinematograph Act of 1952. Its powers are enormous. Not only does it classify films based on the kind of audience that it believes may be permitted to view the picture, but it also enjoys the authority to ban a film altogether on certain specified grounds.

This approach, which gives broad authority to the state to determine which films should be available for broadcasting to the general public, is really symptomatic of the larger culture of censorship in India. In comparison to the role that the state might have played immediately post-independence in the 1950s, there's little to suggest that anything has changed in its approach to censorship. If anything, restrictions on speech have only become more entrenched.

"Censorship is seen as forming an integral part of the state's business," the literary critic and novelist Nilanjana Roy said. "Very few Indians see prior restraint as being opposed to general democratic norms. Indian conservatives would argue that too much free speech is offensive, while Indian liberals would argue that too much free speech is dangerous." →

→ The courts, the supposed guardians of civil liberties, have rarely crushed legislation on the grounds that it violates one's right to free expression. Gautam Bhatia, a lawyer and an expert on free speech legislation, said the last successful challenge against legislation made by parliament on such grounds, before 2015 when the Supreme Court invalidated a provision under India's Information Technology Act, was in 1972. With the courts failing to fulfil their anti-majoritarian functions, the state has had a free reign to impose consistently paternalistic norms.

The present government, headed by the Bharatiya Janata Party's Narendra Modi may go further in restricting speech than earlier regimes. "There is a large amount of cultural policing fundamental to the policies of the BJP government," Nakul Sawhney, an independent filmmaker, said. "Censorship has been present under all regimes in India, but I think the current establishment has a greater tendency to suppress any form of dissent."

Every time the government changes the composition of the CBFC is altered too. The present chairperson, Pahlaj Nihlani, has openly admitted to being a supporter of the government. "I am proud to say I am a BJP person. I believe in [the] BJP," he said on television, after taking office. "Narendra Modi is the voice of the nation. He is my action hero."

Much like the cinema, books too have often been on the receiving end of bans, occasionally expressly by the state, and, in other cases, suppressed by the long arm of the criminal law. In 1988, India became the first country to ban Salman Rushdie's novel, The Satanic Verses. It achieved this by imposing a notification under the Customs Act, prohibiting the import of the book, purportedly on the grounds that it contained blasphemous content.

The Satanic Verses was by no means the only precursor to the more recent bans that the country has seen. There were a significant number of books barred in the years immediately after independence. These included, in 1959, The Heart of India, written by Time Magazine's New Delhi correspondent, Alexander Campbell. The book, a fictional account of Indian bureaucratic life, was banned for its supposedly "repulsive" content.

More recently, works have been proscribed at the bidding of various communities and religions, sometimes at the mere suggestion that a book might contain objectionable content. In 2004, the western Indian state of Maharashtra issued a notification, under India's Code of Criminal Procedure, banning James W. Laine's book Shivaji: Hindu King in Islamic India. The government argued that the book disparaged Shivaji Bhonsle, a 17th-century Marathi leader, who had ousted the Mughals to form a separate state in west India, and, in so doing, had potentially threatened religious sentiments. Eventually, in 2010, the Supreme Court of India found that Laine's book had been illegally banned, in contravention of the constitution's guarantee of free speech and expression.

To approach the courts and to overcome censorship is perhaps the best, and only conceivable technique available for those whose works are thwarted. But, the process can be arduous and time-consuming. What's more, the general record of the courts, both the various high courts and the Supreme Court of India, in preserving the right to free speech, has been poor.

Judges are too often prone to recognising censorship as a legitimate object of the state's functions. In a decision rendered in 2007, the Supreme Court had upheld a notification banning a Kannada novel by PV Narayana on the grounds that certain portions of his book denigrated the character of the sister of an ancient Hindu saint. Even in the absence of any threat of violence, the court held that the burden to disprove the government's objections lay with the novelist.

Article 19(1)(a) of India's Constitution guarantees to its citizens a right to free speech and expression. But the following clause, Article 19(2), permits the state to make "reasonable restrictions" on the right in the interests, among other things, of public order, decency, morality, sovereignty and integrity of the state, friendly relations with foreign states, and so forth. It is this limiting clause, which is often used to justify not only bans on books, but also the operation of various penal provisions that serve to have a chilling effect on speech. "Ultimately, prior restraint as a concept has to be questioned," Pankaj Butalia, a documentary filmmaker, told me. "For that we'll need a movement of great proportions, demanding a change in our constitution."

Both the CBFC and the Film Certification Appellate Tribunal have recently denied Butalia's film, The Textures of Loss, a certificate for screening. One of their ostensible reasons for the decision was the use of the phrase "disproportionate violence" by the filmmaker to describe actions taken by security forces in Kashmir. Another was a statement by one of the interviewees who had recently lost his eight-year-old son because of attacks by Indian security personnel. The father apparently says in the film: "I beg Allah that this kind of an India be damned. That the whole of this India be damned and of our government here and all their families like they've ruined our whole family..."

In January this year, Butalia approached the Supreme Court, seeking to question the standards on which the decision denying him clearance had been made. To his surprise, the judges were more concerned about the broad content of the film than they were with the reasons they had given for censoring it. "Why is [the film] one-sided? Where is the alternate picture? We don't know why it has become fashionable and a question of human rights to talk about one side of a story," justices Vikramjit Sen and Chockalingam Nagappan told the filmmaker. "Rights are always conferred on two parties and not only on one of them... this is what is happening with activists."

Fortunately for Butalia, the justices allowed him to approach the Delhi High Court with a fresh petition challenging the CBFC's decision. On 25 May 2015, the Delhi High Court ruled in favour of the film. It directed the board to grant The Textures of Loss a "U" certificate. But, weeks later, Butalia continued to await permission from the board. He proposes to go to court again, seeking to have the CBFC held in contempt of the courts.

Indian conservatives would argue that too much free speech is offensive, while Indian liberals would argue that too much free speech is dangerous

"The entire censorship regime in India is flawed," Butalia told me. "We can't be expected to rush to the courts each time we want to express ourselves. There's absolutely no hope for an independent voice in our country today." Ganesan, who, like Butalia, is fighting his battle against censorship in the courts, was even more contemptuous of the state of free expression in India. "It doesn't matter which government is in power," he said. "India is a democratic country only in name."

***Subrith Parthasarathy** is a lawyer and writer based in Chennai, India*

Credit: EPA

The books that nobody reads

44(03): 40/42 | DOI: 10.1177/0306422015605712

Iranian satirist **Hadi Khorsandi** was forced into exile after receiving death threats for his work. Over four decades later, he believes censorship has become even harder for Iran's writers to navigate

I WOULD RATHER WRITE about the things that you may not know about Iran: the delights of Persian verse, the vineyards of Shiraz (all dried up because of the teetotal extremists), the wonders of Persepolis and, of course, our food.

Instead, I have to turn to a subject that no one should have to write about in the 21st century: censorship.

A political muzzle for stifling creativity and suppressing truth, censorship, as George Bernard Shaw put it, is "When nobody is allowed to read any books except the books that nobody reads".

That is certainly the case in the Islamic Republic, despite the tireless ingenuity of our censor-skirting, death-dodging poets, writers, filmmakers, journalists and social media commentators.

As I write, the popular humorist Mohammad Reza Ali Payam, affectionately called Haloo, is being transferred from prison to hospital following a hunger strike in response to his mistreatment in jail.

His crime? Light-hearted and mildly critical takes on the unreason of Iran's rulers.

He was imprisoned and released in 2012. In April this year, he was jailed once again on the same trumped-up charges of issuing propaganda and insulting various government officials.

In a YouTube post after the sentencing he said he asked the judge, "For one poem, how many times must I go to jail?" The judge replied: "That's the way it is."

Many believe the real reason for purging secular artists and writers in Iran is the fear of unintended consequences, should those with differing world views operate freely.

Such a policy, one mullah has claimed recently, "would be like assisting the West in destroying our sense of right and wrong from within".

That is why anyone who begins to capture the public imagination, as Ali Payam did with his poetry performances on YouTube, will end up behind bars.

In the past, most authors and artists were more or less familiar with the rules of engagement, and the likes and dislikes of censors. Nowadays censorship in Iran is no longer based on rules. A censor now can decide at whim, what to authorise or refuse.

The only books freely available are those that have to be read by students and scholars. This canon, like all other texts, has been subjected to the most rigorous scrutiny by the shadowy goons of the Ministry of Culture and Islamic Guidance.

And if a book, song, play or film is already out there in the public domain, that's no guarantee for reprints or continued distribution – permissions are revoked arbitrarily.

Writing in The Spectator in 1948, the humorist Paul Jennings jokingly coined the term "resistentialism" – a reference to the struggle between humans and inanimate objects, which, he observed, have a certain power over us.

In the Iranian context the Islamic Republic is that inanimate object – railing against it is like arguing with a shower that only gives you cold water, or willing your iPhone to forgive you after you accidentally pour tea over it.

Conversely, if the Republic sets you in its sights, it can be ruthless in its methods.

In 1995, a bus carrying some two dozen Iranian poets and novelists, who were on their way to a writers' conference in Armenia, veered off-road and into a ravine. It emerged that the driver had deliberately crashed the vehicle, jumping out at the last minute. The "accident" was an assassination attempt. Had it succeeded – the writers survived to tell the tale – practically the entire active literary resistance in Iran would have been wiped out.

He asked the judge, "For one poem, how many times must I go to jail?" The judge replied: "That's the way it is"

In 2012 FATA, a cyber police unit, which enforces the Khomeinist policy of liquidating dissent online, targeted a 35-year-old blogger, Sattar Beheshti. He had used Facebook to describe Iran's justice system as a "slaughterhouse". Beheshti suffered torture before being killed.

Although Beheshti's death caused an international outcry, he was relatively unknown in Iran. So easily threatened is the Khomeinist regime that it nips any sign of dissent in the bud, without mercy, regardless of repercussions at home or abroad.

My friend Ebrahim Harandi, an Iranian writer and psychiatrist based in London, makes a distinction between censorship in a police state and one that is ideologically driven.

"A police state wants a single vision of →

ABOVE-LEFT: A member of the Iranian clergy at the 28th Tehran International Book fair in May 2015

→ the universe and silences challengers," he wrote to me in an email.

"Once this is achieved, others can go about their lives with relative freedom as long as they stay out of politics. States driven by ideology or a creed usually go one step further and wish to police people's thought and their innermost feelings."

Iran's writers and artists are expected to be quiet in public, he said, yet also to explain privately to the authorities what they would like to discuss publicly if they were able to.

Harandi identifies an extensive campaign by Iran's thought police to obtain a "mental map" of each author, with a view to reconfiguring their perspectives and thoughts by whatever means possible.

Authors must avoid positive references to previous regimes while offering a flattering image of the current regime. And every text – even films – must be prefaced by the words: "In the name of God". Those who fail to comply can expect their career to be terminated before long.

Jail, torture and death: these are the Khomeinist regime's prizes for literature.

Thanks to the Board of Censorship under the Ministry of Islamic Guidance in Iran, no one is allowed to write any books, except the books that no one wants to read. ⊗

***Hadi Khorsandi** is an Iranian poet, satirist and political commentator. He editor of the Persian-language satirical journal Asghar Agha, and has lived in the UK since 1979*

CASE STUDY

Writing between the lines

DANIAL HAGHIGHI on a new generation of Iranian writers feeling caught in the censors' trap, and looking for ways to get their voices heard

Young Iranian writers are not allowed to pry into many spaces; there are many red lines that must not be crossed. Religion, politics, public beliefs and even certain social relations are forbidden themes.

Some of the most talented writers I know have migrated to the West, hoping to turn their dreams into another language, become global, and run away from the restrictions. For many, this will lead to disappointment and frustration. Few books by Iranian writers are published in translation.

Those who stay home have the arduous task of trying to get a licence for their books. And a young writer here will struggle to sell 500 copies if they are not backed by propaganda and marketing.

My novel, which I wrote five years ago when I was 21, is about the lifestyle of my generation in Iran today. Its themes include drugs and love. It is banned in Iran, but it can be read on Nogaam.com, which is a Persian-language, self-publishing platform, based in the UK.

Given the predictable threats from institutions of power, not everyone is prepared to take the risk to self-publish. But, in my experience, if you publish your book online, it is better received. People think an unofficial publication is more reliable, as censorship has not stuck its claws in it. The first casualty of censorship is often the reader's trust.

Here in Iran, there is no scarcity of information or knowledge. There are literary NGOs that are hard at work. There are talented writers who can rival their counterparts anywhere in the world. But publishing all that we have achieved is still something we can only wish for; the realisation remains beyond our reach. ⊗

Translated by Daryoush Mohammad Poor

Credit: Eve Arnold/Magnum

ABOVE: Senator Joseph McCarthy at a press conference in 1954

Lessons from McCarthyism

44(03): 43/45 | DOI: 10.1177/0306422015605713

Judith Shapiro, who remembers the impact of McCarthyite accusations on her mother and father, looks at the challenges to free speech in the USA today, and in the past

SIXTY-FIVE YEARS AFTER McCarthyism was coined as the synonym for reckless mud-slinging accusations of communist subversion, it remains the favoured condemnation for practices limiting freedom of expression. US Senator Joseph McCarthy attacked the American left; now it is often Americans left of centre who are accused of "the new McCarthyism" by seeking to suppress "politically incorrect" debates.

The severe and widespread repression of the post-war United States was far more ferocious than today's restrictions. The contemporary pervasive and censorious attacks on individuals for perceived sexism or racism, even when accompanied by Twitter hurricanes, are less numerous and less vicious. Even the reaction to the 9/11 →

→ terrorist attacks, which some defenders of American civil liberties worried would grow into neo-McCarthyism, was very different from the original. McCarthyism saw thousands of people lose their jobs and the imprisonment for years of more than a hundred people – the latter suspected or open members of the US Communist Party sent to jail simply for the ideas they put forward.

Nonetheless, despite this huge gap in severity, some thoughtful American defenders of freedom have argued for the aptness of the equation of the old and new. Distinguished Berkeley statistician Professor Leo Breiman, himself a victim of the original McCarthyism when in the US Army wrote in 2002: "Regretfully, I have come to acknowledge that there is more repression of free speech and free research on my campus than in the McCarthy era."

The point was echoed by retired computer science lecturer Douglas Hainline, who witnessed McCarthyism in his native Texas; he told me: "What makes the current period 'worse' is that it infects the very people who should be most resistant to it. During the 1950s, intelligent people did not buy into McCarthyism even if they kept their heads down".

It is fruitful to compare the various enforcers and instigators of the old and new repression. The role of different arms of government made the old repression particularly vicious; the dominance of civil society activists makes the new repression particularly insidious.

McCarthyism was refined by its namesake, a larger-than-life demagogic individual with a "big lie" to tell and a genius for mainstream media. Yet it was also abetted by government institutions, before and after McCarthy's most powerful years. The less dramatic official government measures, far less well-known today, inflicted much more direct and widespread damage. It was the House Un-American Activities Committee created in the 1930s, not McCarthy, which first attacked Hollywood writers and celebrities, in the clearest censorship of that time. McCarthy came late to the active hunt for "disloyal" communists via US government loyalty boards, a Truman invention which even investigated the patriotism of postmen. Meanwhile, the courts had ruled since World

Credit: Armando L. Sanchez/Alamy

CASE STUDY

Judith Shapiro remembers her parents being investigated

As a child of communist party members growing up in New York City in the McCarthy era, – a so-called "red diaper baby" – I have found the struggle for objectivity on this period a difficult but important goal. My father, a postal worker, faced Truman's loyalty board hearings in 1948 but succeeded in demonstrating that he was not someone who followed the party line during the period of the "Molotov-Ribbentrop" [Hitler-Stalin] Pact, 1939-1941. Clearly a maverick, he had put forward trade union resolutions to open a second front in Europe at the time that the communist party was calling the war in Europe a "phoney war". My mother, a social worker in New York City and a member of the "communist-dominated" United Public Workers, was fired from her job. I remember banner headlines in the New York City tabloids, about the successful purge of "reds" from the city's Department of Public Welfare, and the journalists "doorstepping" her, a junior party member. I was also, by what has always seemed to me a strange coincidence, at the age of six, a witness to the pivotal Paul Robeson concert and Peekskill riots described in the main story. We had a modest summer rental there, and attended the first concert. I was much put out that for my physical protection I was not

War I that a "clear and present danger" allowed the curtailment of free speech – a provision that was not revised until 1969.

McCarthyism could not have survived without popular support; there was widespread acceptance that communists had disqualified themselves from the protection of civil liberties just by being communists. Indeed, in 1949 at Peekskill, ordinary people rioted to disrupt a concert by the great black communist singer Paul Robeson. Yet the predominant role was played by the three branches of government.

Thus does McCarthyism differ from the new repression, in which the leading role is played by "the very people who should be most resistant to it". Some (not all) activists for women's and black equality in the US clearly believe that those who have offensive views should be denied freedom of speech, thoroughly oblivious to the precedent they are setting.

If we focus only on the most serious consequences of McCarthyism to individuals, then further censorship in the present seems much less threatening. If the damage is measured by a less fearful but more universal self-censorship then the comparison is imprecise, but clearly valid.

The sides have changed, but the idea that free speech is a commodity which can easily be traded away is common to both unhappy periods. In less calm times it is too late to plant the idea that freedom of expression is first of all for those whose ideas we think most repugnant, and too late for it to grow roots. If we decide that we will defeat these ideas by suppression, it soon becomes a habit. ⊗

© *Judith Shapiro*

***Judith Shapiro** is an undergraduate tutor at the London School of Economics*

ABOVE: One of the protesters at the University of Illinois demonstrates in support of Professor Steven Salaita. In 2014, Salaita had the offer of a professorial position at the university withdrawn after posting tweets that criticised Israeli policyß

allowed to attend the second.

I also listened to the Army-McCarthy hearings the following year on the radio, perhaps just because my parents' attention was so riveted on them. I understood the triumph they represented. Attacks on the slowly growing civil rights movement in the US southern states were part of this picture. Yet I also became aware that I should not sign petitions or join organisations, even before I had left primary school. The world seemed to change dramatically and suddenly as we entered the 1960s. To some extent the 1960s were a backlash against the 1950s.

The times seem so different now, and conformity in the US so much less that we joke that nonconformity is the new conformity. This is a reason why the new McCarthyism may be less damaging – Americans can retreat to their side of the fence and comfort zone. In the 1950s there was no place to retreat – except sometimes abroad if they had not taken away your passport. The FBI often followed you to your new employment.

Yet the common failure to place freedom of speech high enough on anyone's agenda is a worrisome signal that a new difficult period could again ignite a more massive witch hunt. The possible emergence of a new Cold War and of growing economic insecurity shows us the risks, even if they are not yet a "clear and present danger". Yet methods to combat censorship must take on the voluntary double burden of scrupulously avoiding suppression of the would-be censors.

JS

Doxxed

44(03): 46/49 | DOI: 10.1177/0306422015605714

When prominent women express their views online, they can face a torrent of misogynist abuse. **Brianna Wu**, who was targeted during the Gamergate scandal, gives her view

Dominic Lipinski/PA

LEFT: Women who are outspoken online can face a barrage of hate mail, including threats of rape, murder and doxxing, which is when personal details are revealed

What is Gamergate?

A targeted sexist attack on women in the videogame world began in August 2014, soon manifesting in a Twitter hashtag, #Gamergate. Anonymous trolls gathered on online forums such as Reddit, 4chan and 8chan, where some issued threats of doxxing, rape and death towards female developers, with Zoe Quinn and Brianna Wu among the primary targets.

YOU LEARN TO expect it: the death threats and personal attacks that come with being a woman on the internet. You might even expect being "doxxed" – having your personal details leaked online, an increasingly common technique used by trolls and hackers to silence people they don't agree with.

If you're a high-profile woman like me, you have to constantly ask yourself if your post will put you or your loved ones in danger. After 150 death threats, after people have called your private phone while masturbating, after the stories written about your murder, you worry. You ask yourself if pictures taken will give away addresses, you worry about your pets when you leave your house. Knowing that hate-speech sites continually monitor everything you tweet or write, you constantly second-guess everything you say publicly.

My name is Brianna Wu. I'm a software engineer and head of development at Giant Spacekat, a Boston-based independent games studio. Sometimes, when I'm not making videogames, I have opinions about working in one of the most notoriously sexist fields in the world. For this, I am regularly called a liar, a bitch and a fraud – and those are just the names I laugh off.

It's a familiar pattern for any woman who works in this industry. A friend of mine just published a game review on one of the biggest sites in the world. Her article has 600 comments, and she's terrified of what personal attacks lurk there. Another friend had an armed Special Weapons Attack Team sent to her house after someone falsely reported her for criminal activity. Another friend had pictures of her →

LEGAL GUIDELINES

"US law protects against violence and threats"

By GREG LUKIANOFF

As a US first amendment lawyer, I am surprised to meet people who believe that free speech is out of control, and that the law doesn't protect those attacked online.

I have to assure them that not all speech is protected by the first amendment to the US constitution. Important exceptions include threats of violence, intimidation, harassment, incitement, and libel. And practices such as falsely reporting people to the police so that SWAT teams descend on their homes (a practice dubbed "swatting") are certainly not protected for a bevy of reasons.

What US law does have, however, is a strong presumption that statements of opinion are protected, even when hateful or insulting. The US Supreme Court has said that a "bedrock principle" of the first amendment is that offensiveness alone cannot render speech unprotected. (That language comes from a case in which burning the US flag was ruled to be constitutionally protected expression.)

The US first amendment draws a sharp distinction between speech and action. While some legal scholars argue that the boundary is fuzzy, it's usually not that hard to discern. Harassment, for example, is not so much considered an exception to the first amendment's protection of speech. Rather, it's prohibited as a pattern of directed, discriminatory conduct severe and pervasive enough to harm a reasonable person.

Threats in US law are always contextual. ("Say hello to your mother for me" means something different coming from your auntie than it does from a serial killer.) The 2003 Supreme Court case Virginia v Black provides a useful illustration of where the line between protected and unprotected speech/expression is drawn. The case concerned a state law prohibiting cross burning, a tactic used by the Ku Klux Klan to intimidate black families. The law regarded any and all cross burning as presumptive evidence of an intent to unlawfully intimidate others.

The court struck down the law on first amendment grounds. Sometimes, the court found, burning a cross was an attempt to intimidate – but not always. When burned at a Klan rally, the cross served as a symbol of solidarity, albeit a hateful one. A state could lawfully ban the burn-

→ children posted in a paedophile forum.

We all committed the same crime: in the course of our professional lives, we had an opinion and we voiced it. The UK journalist Laurie Penny famously said: "A woman's opinion is the short skirt of the internet. Having one and flaunting it is somehow asking an amorphous mass of almost-entirely male keyboard-bashers to tell you how they'd like to rape, kill and urinate on you."

It's time to have an adult conversation about how people experience "free speech" on the internet when you are not white, straight, or male. The truth is there is no free speech when speaking about your experiences leads to death threats, doxxing and having armed police sent to your house. And yet asking institutions to respond to these kinds of abuses is taken by some to be ushering in an Orwellian state.

The reality is online spaces are not safe for women. I believe some communities deal with it better than others. The photo-sharing network Pinterest has one of the best records, while Twitter has one of the worst. ("We suck at dealing with abuse," wrote the Twitter CEO, Dick Costolo, in a memo leaked in February.) These online spaces are the public squares of 2015, where we make professional contacts, hang out with our friends and make meaningful connections.

ing of a cross to convey a threat of violence, but could not ban someone from burning a cross in their own backyard solely because it communicated a bad point of view. Because the law failed to distinguish between different possible contexts and purposes, it violated the first amendment. Simply, expressing an offensive idea is protected, conveying a threat is not.

The court defined unlawful intimidation as "a type of true threat, where a speaker directs a threat to a person or group of persons with the intent of placing the victim in fear of bodily harm or death". Threats of other illegal retaliation are likewise not protected.

Harsh online expression is often protected under the US first amendment, but many horrifying examples concern speech that is not protected. Threats, libel and intimidation are prohibited, as are any number of crimes (such as extortion, invasion of privacy, or fraud) where the fact that words are used to commit a crime is no defence. ⊗

Greg Lukianoff *is president of the Foundation for Individual Rights in Education and author of Unlearning Liberty (Encounter Books)*

Public efforts by feminists, racial-equality advocates and gay-rights leaders to communicate community concerns are met with outright hostility.

The war between free-speech absolutism and those calling for protection against vicious harassment has recently put the future of the Reddit network in question. The 10th most trafficked site in the US, billing itself as "the front page" of the internet, Reddit is favoured by particular types of internet users. More than 60 per cent are under 26; 74 per cent are male. Samantha Allen of the Daily Beast described Reddit as not so much a front page as a "spacious, tricked-out man cave".

Reddit has become one of the most toxic, abusive places online. It is one of the largest homes of organised white supremacy on the internet. Reddit users have enthusiastically defended forums such as /r/rapingwomen as their God-given right. They worry that blocking /r/fatpeoplehate, a Reddit community dedicated to publicly mocking and harassing overweight people, was akin to government censure. Many of the racists and misogynists have since taken their toys and gone to 8chan and Voat, sites where there is little or no moderation.

A friend had an armed SWAT team sent to her house after someone falsely reported her for criminal activity

It should probably be a relief that the forces of organised harassment, such as Gamergate [see sidebar], can rarely respond to our ideas. So they attack our looks instead. The value that brings to open speech isn't a gain: it's a huge loss, as many of us learn it's easier to stay silent. Death threats bring nothing to a conversation; nor do attacks on a woman's looks or racist insults. ⊗

Brianna Wu is a videogames developer from the US, and the founder of Giant Spacekat (giantspacekat.com)

Glossing over the bad news

44(03): 50/51 | DOI: 10.1177/0306422015605715

Rob Hutton presents a glossary of verbal political props from the Newspeak of today, and decodes them

WHY BOTHER WITH censorship? It's so much effort, with the firewalls, and the monitoring, and the prisons. Honestly guys (and you know who you are), you'd be much better off sticking to rebranding.

For instance, if your opponent is raising money in a way you don't like, why not call it a "stealth tax"? It doesn't even need to be a tax. In Britain, one of the Labour Party's few achievements over the last five years was to successfully name a welfare cut "the bedroom tax". After a while, that was even the name government officials used.

In the 20th century, the USSR "resettled" the Kulaks, wealthy peasants, beyond the Urals, and they were "liquidated as a class". If a relative was arrested, and you were told they had "no right of correspondence", it was because they had been shot.

When Soviet satellite states showed signs of moving too far towards democracy, they were given "fraternal assistance": the tanks were sent in. President Putin would insist Russia today is only "fraternally" trying to protect Ukraine – while protecting the homeland from "foreign agents" (aka NGOs) and its "traditional values" from "gay propaganda" (universal human-rights claims).

So, in the hope of weaning oppressive states on to a more civilised method of thought control, here's your handy glossary of words and phrases that can mean a little more or less than you think:

- DEMOCRATIC: when it appears in a country's name, "totalitarian"; as in the German Democratic Republic, the Democratic People's Republic of Korea and the Democratic Republic of the Congo.
- DIKTAT: statement with which I disagree.
- DOSSIER: any collection of allegations that we have written down.
- EXTENDED READINESS: used by the Royal Navy to describe ships, "mothballed".
- GIMMICK: a popular idea we wish we'd thought of.
- IDEOLOGICAL: someone with fixed ideas whom we dislike; if we do like them, try "committed".
- IMPOSED: the means by which things of which we disapprove are implemented.
- INDUSTRIAL: the scale on which bad things have been happening.
- MORE WIDELY: where we need to look for answers, because we don't like the ones we've found in the places we've looked so far.
- PER SE: ignore what I just said; as in, "we have no plans, per se".
- PLAYING POLITICS: an irregular verb, conjugated as follows: I am raising an important issue, you are scoring points, he is playing politics.

Credit: Shutterstock

- **PROJECTING FORCE**: attacking other countries.
- **PUBLIC DIPLOMACY**: propaganda.
- **REGIME**: government with which we disagree.
- **TECHNOCRAT**: someone who understands the subject, but whom I wish you to ignore; antonym: 'independent expert'.
- **WE MUST FOCUS ON THE IMMEDIATE ISSUE**: and not the thing you keep asking about.
- **WE NEED A GROWN-UP DEBATE**: I will only engage with people who agree with me.
- **WE NEED TO LOOK MORE WIDELY**: until we find some evidence that supports my conclusions.
- **WE RULE NOTHING OUT**: we're ruling lots of things out, including the thing you just said, but this isn't the moment to tell you.

Robert Hutton *covers British politics for Bloomberg News. He is the author of Would They Lie To You? How To Spin Friends And Influence People, and Romps, Tots and Boffins: The Strange Language of News*

Reporting rights?

44(03): 52/55 | DOI: 10.1177/0306422015605716

In a series of interviews with journalists in the former Yugoslavia, **Milana Knezevic** reports on the new elites in control, death threats, and the legacy of the post-war period of the early 2000s

TODAY THE BULK of the media in the Balkans has "been bought by people with no history in, or understanding of, the media business; they promote narrow interests of their owners or new political elites; sometimes without even pretence of objectivity," said Kemal Kurspahic, former editor of Oslobodjenje, an independent newspaper published during the Bosnian war, reflecting on the development of media freedom over the past 25 years.

While in the 1990s nationalism was the order of the day, today a whole host of challenges – including murky media ownership – face independent journalists across the region. The Balkan Investigative Journalism Network in Serbia, for instance, has documented the campaign against them from authorities and pro-government press on a dedicated website, BIRN Under Fire. Television journalist Jet Xharra and BIRN Kosovo took the government to court over the right to report on the prime minister's accounts, and to set a legal precedent for press freedom in the state. But Xharra, country director of BIRN in Kosovo, said there is a sense of disbelief among those who had to report during war, that these kinds of battles still need to be fought.

"We cannot understand why, 20 years later, you have to deal with [such] a strain on your reporting," said Xharra.

During the war years that tore Yugoslavia apart, press freedom, like pretty much every other aspect of society, experienced a profound crisis. Large swathes of the media in the former republics became propaganda tools for ruling elites, even before the fighting started. In fact, concerted media campaigns of hate and fear-mongering played an important part in priming people who had lived side by side for decades for war. As British historian Mark Thompson put it in his 1999 book Forging War, on the media's role in the conflicts in Bosnia, Croatia and Serbia: "War is the continuation of television news by other means."

Yet during the Balkan wars beginning in the 1990s there were local journalists who, in the face of enormous pressure, rejected nationalist and propagandist lines, and attempted to sift truth from lies and distortion. Beyond the daily struggle that came with just existing in a war zone, independent journalism was dangerous work. As Human Rights Watch points out in a new report on the state of media freedom in the Balkans, journalists who were, at the time, "critical of official government positions were often labelled as traitors or spies working on behalf of foreign interests and against the state".

Serbia's B92, a rare dissenting voice in a media landscape shaped by President Slobodan Milosevic's propaganda strategy, is perhaps the most famous example of independent journalism. Set up in 1989 as a

Credit: Reuters

ABOVE: People reading Bosnian daily Oslobodjenje in front of the newspaper's war-damaged office building in Sarajevo in 2001

youth-focused radio station (later branching out into TV and web platforms), B92 bravely covered a turbulent time – from the war in Bosnia, to the Nato bombing of Serbia, to the protest movement that eventually saw Milošević ousted. For this, it was continuously hounded by the government. At one point in 1999 authorities commandeered its offices and radio frequency, forcing the station off air, before it could resume broadcasting from a different studio and frequency, under the name B2-92.

In Croatia, President Franjo Tudjman also made sure ultra-nationalism had a place in column inches and on airwaves. Feral Tribune, which started out in 1983 as a satirical supplement in the newspaper Slobodna Dalmacija, had other ideas. Under sustained pressure from the authorities, it covered stories of human rights and conflict that many other outlets avoided, in addition to its biting satire. It was taken to court, publicly burned, and one journalist was even drafted into the army after Feral published an edited photo of Tudjman and Milosevic in bed together on the front page.

Bosnia was the country in the region that would be by far the hardest hit by fighting. But even as war came to Sarajevo, independent journalism survived in some small way. Oslobodjenje, which started out as an anti-Nazi paper in 1943, had a track record of editorial independence. In 1988, staff for the first time voted for their own editor – Kemal Kurspahić – instead of accepting one appointed by the authorities. Just three years later they fought for their freedom again, this time in the constitutional court, as the newly elected nationalist parties agreed to adopt a law whereby they could appoint the editors and managers of Bosnian media. In 1992 came their toughest challenge yet. With the two towers of their office building under fire – in one night they lost six floors on one side and four on the other – they decided to go underground, and continue their work from a nuclear bomb shelter, with no newsprint supplies and no phone links. →

MAPPING FREEDOM

Dangers of reporting in the Balkans

Attacks on journalists and journalism in the Balkans, compiled from Index's Mapping Media Freedom project

SERBIA

Independent online news outlet Pescanik has been targeted on several occasions after reporting in June 2014 that a senior minister had plagiarised parts of his doctoral dissertation. The site has faced distributed denial-of-service (DDoS) attacks, and hackers have altered text and blocked IP addresses, thus preventing readers from accessing content.

MONTENEGRO

In May 2015, after reporting on corruption in local government, journalist Milovan Novovic's car was vandalised. In June, journalist Alma Ljuca's car was attacked in a similar way. This comes after a car belonging to the daily Vijesti was torched in early 2014.

BOSNIA

In December 2014, police raided the Sarajevo offices of news site Klix.ba, looking for a recording in which the prime minister of the country's Republika Srpska entity spoke about "buying off" politicians. This came after the site's director and a journalist were interrogated and asked to reveal their source for the recording, which they refused to do.

CROATIA

In May 2015, journalist and blogger Željko Peratović was attacked by three men outside his home, and hospitalised with head injuries. Peratović is known for his investigative reporting, and has covered the trial of two agents of the former Yugoslav Security Agency.

MACEDONIA

Deputy Prime Minister for Economic Affairs Vladimir Peshevski was filmed physically assaulting Sashe Ivanovski, a journalist and owner of the news site Maktel, who has been critical of the government.

SLOVENIA

In March 2015 photojournalist Jani Bozic received a suspended prison sentence for publishing a photo of Alenka Bratusek, then prime minster elect, which showed him receiving a congratulatory text message from a prominent businessman 20 minutes before results were announced.

KOSOVO

Express journalist Visar Duriqi, who has covered radical Islamists in Kosovo, has received a number of death threats, including threats of beheading. ⊗

Index on Censorship's Mapping Media Freedom project (mappingmediafreedom.org) launched in 2014 to record threats to media freedom throughout the European Union and EU candidate countries. It has recently expanded to cover Russia and Ukraine.

MK

→ "If dozens of foreign journalists could come to report on the siege of Sarajevo and Bosnian war, how could we – whose families, city and country were under attack – stop doing our job?" Kurspahic, now managing editor of Connection Newspapers, told Index. They felt an obligation to their readers: "We could not leave them without news at the worst time of their lives."

Oslobodjenje even celebrated its 50th anniversary during the war, with 82 papers around the world printing some of their stories. With that they achieved "the ultimate victory", Kurspahic said, "if the aim of the terror against Oslobodjenje was to silence us as a voice of multiethnic Bosnia".

"People were getting killed, so we were reporting it. The risk was physical at that time to journalists," Xharra told Index. Today she hosts Kosovo's most watched current affairs programme, as well as fulfilling her role at BIRN Kosovo. But she cut her reporting teeth as a translator, fixer and field producer for UK broadcasters – the BBC and Channel 4 – during the Kosovo war. She recalled going through frontlines for a story, and hiding tapes from paramilitary checkpoints, painting a vivid picture of a time when practicing journalism in the western Balkans meant near constant risk of physical harm.

Journalists could be caught in crossfire, or targeted specifically for their work. Kurspahic remembers the Oslobodjenje reporter Kjasif Smajlovic in Zvornik, who sent his wife and children away, and stayed to report on the fall of the town until he was killed by Serbian paramilitary forces in April 1992. In 1999, Slavko Curuvija, known for his critical reporting, was shot 17 times in a Belgrade side street, just days after a pro-government daily had labelled him a Nato supporter. In many cases, there has been little to no accountability for such crimes, breeding a culture of impunity that still hangs over the region.

Because while the darkest days for press freedom in the Balkans came during wartime, peace has not brought the improved conditions many hoped for. At a talk in March, Dunja Mijatovic, the OSCE's free expression representative, went as far as to say that the situation now is worse than in the aftermath of the conflicts.

And today the media itself remains part of the problem, especially when journalists turn on their colleagues. One prominent example is the story of BIRN Serbia. Following their critical investigation into a state-owned power company, Prime Minister Aleksandar Vucic labelled the group liars who had been funded by the EU to speak against his government. That attack was then taken forward by the pro-government Serbian press, including in the newspaper Informer. Just one example where the media has been a less than staunch defender of its own rights.

Data from Index's Mapping Media Freedom project, which tracks media freedom across Europe, indicates that worries of threats to media rights are justified. In just over a year it has received more than 170 reports of violations from the countries of

Newspaper staff continued their work from a nuclear bomb shelter, with no newsprint supplies and no phone links

the former Yugoslavia. Incidents included a Croatian journalist who received a letter saying she would "end up like Curuvija"; a Bosnian journalist threatened over Facebook by a local politician; Kosovan journalists depicted as animals on several billboards; a Montenegrin daily that had a company car torched; a Macedonian editor who had a funeral wreath sent to his home; and a Slovenian who faced charges for reporting on the intelligence agency. Online and offline, physical and verbal, serious threats to press freedom remain, some 20 years on.

***Milana Knezevic** was born in the former Yugoslavia and is the former assistant online editor of Index on Censorship. She tweets @milanaknez*

My life on the blacklist

44(03): 56/58 | DOI: 10.1177/0306422015605717

After the fall of the Soviet Union, Uzbek writer **Mamadali Makhmudov** expected to be acclaimed for writing critically about Russia, but instead he found himself persecuted even more

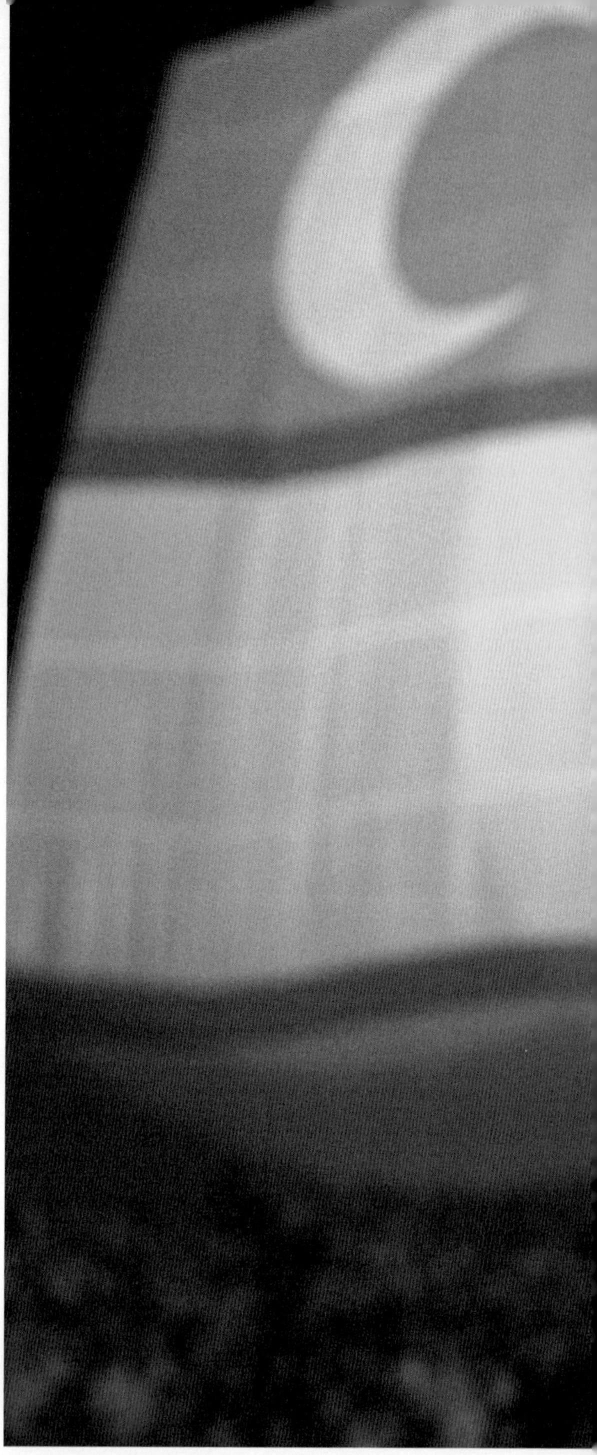

Credit: Reuters/ Shamil Zhumatov

"BRAVO, BRAVO", "LONG live ...", "the great, the incomparable." All these hollow, deceitful words fill up the newspapers and magazines of Uzbekistan. As far as I can see, our media is still bound by the ghosts of the Soviet Union. The exaggerated greatness of the establishment feels like a mouse being shown in the shape of an elephant.

During Soviet times, I used to work at state magazines and newspapers. The censorship then was immense and undeniable. Every news report or article, novella or novel, was written according to socialist realism: it praised the Soviet regime, the Communist Party, its leader, and big brother, meaning the Russian people. Any journalist or writer who didn't follow these strict orders was an enemy of the people.

The censor would sieve through every single last word, and only then allow publication. If any sentence or thought didn't follow the censor's requirements, you would never see it in the press, and the author would find him or herself blacklisted. I was on this blacklist.

In 1981, when my short novel Olmez Kayalar (Immortal Cliffs) was serialised in Shark Yildizi magazine, the KGB sacked everyone who had allowed the book to reach publication. The novel was about the history of Uzbeks fighting against Russian colonisation: a theme considered taboo by the establishment. I was placed under enormous pressure. Officers of the KGB, who used to call themselves "special workers", followed me everywhere, and sometimes

they would invite me back to Tashkent hotels – called Russia and Leningrad – where they had "special rooms" allocated to them.

I do remember one particular occasion, when a Russian KGB officer, called Anatoly, bombarded me with questions: "Why did you write Immortal Cliffs in spite of socialist realism? Why are there no Russian characters in your novel? Why is there no praise for the great Russian people who brought development and progress to Turkestan?"

It was an especially frightening time for me. A time of fear. A time of death. I lived thinking: what should I do? Should I escape? But to where could I escape, even if I tried? Should I commit suicide? Yet what about my family and my children?

This "special officer" Anatoly attempted to understand my situation. He strongly suggested I co-operate by reworking the novel. "I'll give you time," he said. "You know, for you to add the chapters about the progressive role of Russia in Turkestan ... to show that a rotten, backward, poor, figuratively dead country, was transformed into a place of culture, education, science, technology." →

ABOVE: A soldier stands in front of Uzbekistan's national flag during an Independence Day celebration in Tashkent

RIGHT: Uzbek novelist Mamadali Makhmudov, who was in prison for 14 years

→ I kept silent. Anatoly continued to pressurise me into accepting his ideas.

Luckily for me, I knew the first secretary of the Communist Party of Uzbekistan, Sharaf Rashidov – a prominent author himself – who spoke personally to Leonid Brezhnev, the general secretary of the Central Committee of the Communist Party of the Soviet Union. This saved me from imprisonment and I was sent to a Moscow writers' resort to re-edit the novel.

When my short novel was serialised in a magazine, the KGB sacked everyone who had allowed the book to reach publication

After this incident, I started to write mini-stories that even the censor wouldn't understand, for instance:

A Horse

A rider shakes his reins, whilst whipping his horse. A skinny Qorabayir [the name of the Horse] is pelting along: sometimes right or left; sometimes straight or skewing diagonally. The poor creature is sweating uncontrollably, panting and unable to breathe. The rider pays the creature no attention, whipping the horse in the head, and kicking it in the belly with no remorse. Tears trickle from the eyes of the horse, with foam gathering at its mouth. The animal is on its last legs, struggling at the brink of collapse, yet cannot bear to disappoint the rider.

After the breakup of the Soviet Union, when the ideas of national sovereignty and independence that I so prominently described in my novel became the state's ideology, I expected to be recognised and even honoured. Alas, the opposite happened. I was arrested twice and imprisoned. The second time I was sent to jail for 14 years.

Campaigns by Pen International and other human right organisations, for which I am very grateful, helped achieve my release in 2013, after long years of humiliation, torture and suffering. I am free now, yet I'm not totally free.

My associates and I have tried many times to publish my literary works. Even the works that I wrote during the Soviet times are not accepted by any newspaper, magazine or publishing house in Uzbekistan. All of them consider me a blacklisted writer, and none of them want to be associated with me.

It's not just that there is no publisher for my political writing in my homeland; I can't even find a publisher in Uzbekistan for my historic novels or short stories.

Censorship of the media in Uzbekistan is the enemy of development. It hacks away at the roots of justice and kills the truth. In order to raise the level of the media, we need a new generation of talented young people, independent minds, who love their nation and motherland more than themselves. They should work not for money, but to sow the seeds of truth to their fellow citizens even if the price they pay is to sacrifice themselves. I pray to my creator simply for that. ⊗

Mamadali Makhmudov is an award-winning writer, based in Uzbekistan. He was released from prison in 2013, aged 72, after serving 14 years on charges of plotting to overthrow the constitutional government

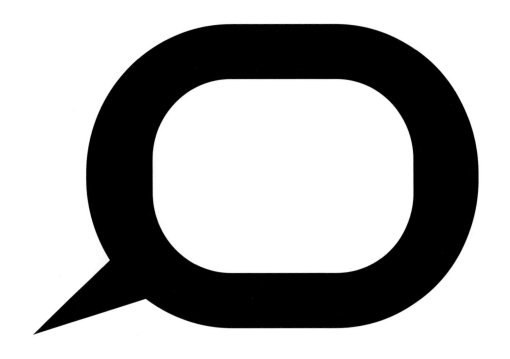

Credit: Vaclav Havel Library / Ondrej Nemec

GLOBAL VIEW

44(03): 60/61 | DOI: 10.1177/0306422015605718

Libraries are an incredible resource for communities, for increasing knowledge and for freedom of expression. They are needed for the future as much as the past, argues **Jodie Ginsberg**

I WAS SITTING IN a library when I first had a discussion – via email – about the possibility of working for Index. I was in the biographies section, researching a paper on payments systems (there were no seats in the finance section), when an email pinged into my inbox asking if I might be interested in applying for a new job. I looked up from my computer and instantly spotted a biography of someone with the same name as the man who had just written to me. It's not a common surname. It felt like an omen.

Libraries do that. They exert a very special kind of magic. As a child, I think it was a combination of the silence and the feeling of being on a constant treasure hunt that made a visit to the library so special. As an adult, it was the mystery of wandering along dimly lit corridors in buildings that felt like labyrinths. Libraries hold out the magic of discovery: new writers, new pictures, new worlds. Digital databases cannot replicate the excitement of uncovering something special, such as the two pages from the Koran, thought to be more than 1,400 years old and found hidden in a book in the University of Birmingham's library in July.

Our library at Index is much smaller and takes up just one wall (although we're running out of shelves), but treasures still occasionally tumble from the pages of our archived magazines: notes from former editors, a copy signed by writer and former president of Czechoslovakia Václav Havel, a letter from playwright Alan Bennett, photographs from the film premiere of Ariel Dorfman's Death and the Maiden, which was held as an Index fundraiser. So far, no great undiscovered manuscripts have been unearthed but we live in hope.

Libraries offer the possibility of discovery for many reasons, not least because they should be places where censorship is left at the door. Sadly, this is not always the case. Between 5,099 challenges were reported to the Office for Intellectual Freedom in the last decade

The American Library Association estimates that around 300 books are removed or challenged in US schools and libraries every year – although this is likely to be only a fraction of the total as many book bans are never reported. It is vital that as libraries adapt and change, resistance to censorship remains at the heart of their mission.

Because libraries are changing. These are no longer just hallowed halls of quiet study. They are also increasingly becoming places where individuals come to share knowledge, to discuss it, to question it, and to celebrate it. The British Library received criticism recently for redeveloping its space and becoming more like a giant "students' union". Instead of having the intimidating entrance halls of many great libraries, the redesigned British Library now offers sofas and free Wi-Fi to reflect the changing needs of readers.

The British Council, after a long period of closing down its libraries, is building new ones in south Asia, recognising that the libraries are not just important repositories of knowledge, but also offer rare spaces for individuals to meet and discuss books and ideas in an apolitical space. "Libraries have always been at the heart of the communities they serve," the British Council's Tomas Doherty wrote ahead of the reopening of the British Council library in Dhaka last year. It's a view echoed by author Joanne Harris, who has written of libraries as "a civic space that bind communities" and called for more public money to be spent on them.

According to the Bill & Melinda Gates Foundation, there are more than 320,000 libraries worldwide, 73 per cent of them in developing and transitioning countries. As the organisation notes, in many communities, public libraries are the only place where any person, regardless of education or skill level, can have access to information and the internet, free of charge.

Libraries are the only place where any person, regardless of education or skill level, can have access to information, free of charge

The reinvention of libraries is necessary in the face of public funding cuts, but it also reflects a change in behaviour, as people look not just to accumulate knowledge but to share it too. Even the Index library is part of this trend. Our library has hosted dissidents, MPs, authors, illustrators, activists – even parties. It is a place where anyone can talk freely and without fear, where knowledge is shared and discoveries are made. We just need more shelves. ⊗

Jodie Ginsberg is the CEO of Index on Censorship

LEFT: Participants at The Cat That Never Sleeps, an event held at the Václav Havel Library in Prague. As well as holding a huge collection of archive material by Vaclav Havel, the library hosts numerous events

IN FOCUS

In this section

MAIN: Residents wearing masks pose for a hazy photograph near a statue of the late Chairman of the People's Republic of China Mao Zedong in Xinjiang. Hundreds of posts relating to Under the Dome, a documentary about air pollution in China, were removed from microblogging platform Weibo when the documentary first aired in March 2015

Credit: China Stringer Network/Reuters

Battle of the bans

44(03): 64/66 | DOI: 10.1177/0306422015605719

US author **Judy Blume** talks to **Vicky Baker** about parents' and teachers' overly protective attitudes to young people's feelings, and how she has spent the last 45 years tackling bans and censorship

"**WHY DID YOU** kill the pet turtle?" The question took author Judy Blume by surprise on a recent US book tour. The child asking it was referring to a novel first published in 1972, Tales of a Fourth Grade Nothing, where Dribble, the pet turtle, is accidentally swallowed by the protagonist's younger brother. "I'd never heard that complaint before," Blume told Index on a recent trip to the UK. "People found it funny before, but now I can expect animals-have-feelings-too complaints. Those sorts of questions strike you as funny, but it's awful too. It's the adults behind them that are the problem."

Blume, who has sold 80 million books and been translated into 32 languages, has nothing against turtles, or indeed children's attachment to pets. But she talks of the "new, very protective" approach to reading that she is seeing more and more. "It's the job of a parent to help children deal with unexpected things that happen," said the Florida-based writer, best known for her teen titles. "I often get letters saying, 'We didn't like it when this thing happened in your book, so we're not going to read any of them again.'"

By tackling coming-of-age issues, including sex and puberty, she has experienced various cries of outrage along the way, as well as outright bans by some schools and libraries. In 2009, her publisher even had to send her a bodyguard, after she was deluged with hate-mail and threats for speaking out in support of Planned Parenthood, a US pro-choice group. Five Judy Blume books feature in the 100 most frequently challenged list (1990 to 1999), compiled by the American Library Association, which tracks attempts to ban or censor literature, often by US school boards.

Like many people, I grew up with Judy. I was 11 by the time I had devoured most of her back catalogue. I remember a battered paperback of Forever – the infamous teen sex novel – being passed around my class like contraband, although all our parents and teachers must have known we had it. Her writing about periods was far more enlightening than anything we were taught at school. I still remember the nurse who came into our class and frightened the hell out of us by waving a super-size tampon in the air. "My mum has those!" one school friend said proudly. Her mum was French. I was sure mine didn't mess with such things.

A US website, Flavorwire, recently compiled a list of "awkward Judy Blume moments" from people's youth. There was one where a local librarian lent her eight-year-old grandson the novel about a girl's first period and he wept at the sheer horror of it. There was another about a nine-year-old who had a public tantrum and screamed "Censorship!" at the top of her voice when told she was "not ready" for Judy. Perhaps

Credit: Elena Seibert

ABOVE: Author Judy Blume has sold 80 million books, but has seen numerous calls for her titles for young adults to be banned

the most enlightening, however, was the person who admitted trying to get Are You There God? It's Me, Margaret removed from the library because she thought it questioned the existence of God. "I didn't read it until years later, far past the time when my fundamentalism had lapsed," she confessed, inadvertently playing a part in the long tradition that sees the most vocal criticism of books coming from those who haven't read them.

"I've always said censorship is caused by fear," Blume told Index, while on tour to launch her latest book In the Unlikely Event. As a board member of the National Coalition Against Censorship in the US, she has long spoken with passion about her views on the freedom to read, and against books being censored.

Among the most recent children's books to be targeted in the US are Jeanette Winter's The Librarian of Basra and Nasreen's Secret School, which are based on true stories from Iraq and Afghanistan, respectively. Parents from Florida's Duval County created a petition in July to object to the books references to Islam and war.

"I don't use age ratings. There's no reason why someone who wants to, can't read it. I don't believe in saying books are for certain age groups," said Blume, when asked, at a recent UK event at King's Place, London, if she thought her newest book, written for adults, should be restricted to readers of a certain age.

If censorship had an agony aunt, it would be Blume. Throughout her long career, she's tackled the big issue openly and without judgement. "Am I being a censor?" a mother asked her recently, after confessing she omitted a section of Tales of a Fourth Grade Nothing when she read it to her children. It was a segment where a father is left in charge of his two sons and makes a real hash of it by not knowing how to handle them. "The mother decided not to read that part to her own boys, because she didn't want them to know how other dads are," said Blume. "That's your choice. But my advice is read it all. Talk about it, laugh about it. Say: 'Aren't we glad our dad is different?' No, it's not censorship. It's your decision. But are you going to do them any favours by trying to protect them?"

And then comes the thing that makes Blume "very, very upset": trigger warnings. These are cautions put on books or reading lists to warn of potentially upsetting content, and they are becoming a growing practice at US colleges. Blume only came across the term recently, but instantly took it very seriously. "Why do college students need to be warned that what they are about to read might make them feel bad? These are 20-year-olds, but they need a professor to warn them? →

FACTFILE

Judy Blume and censorship

By MAX GOLDBART

1 Judy Blume's Forever is ranked seventh in the 100 most challenged books, 1990-1999, by the American Library Association. Other Blume books on the list are Deenie, Are You There God? It's Me Margaret, Tiger Eyes and Blubber.
2 Blume was once phoned and accused of being a communist for writing Are You There God? It's Me, Margaret, even though the book has nothing to do with politics.
3 In a 1993 article for Index on Censorship magazine, Blume wrote: "My book Blubber was banned in Montgomery County, Maryland, for 'lack of moral tone' and, more recently, challenged in Canton, Ohio, for allowing evil behaviour to go unpunished. Yet in New Zealand it is used in teacher-training classes to help explain classroom dynamics."
4 Are You There God? It's Me Margaret was removed from elementary school libraries in Gilbert, Arizona in 1980 and parental consent was required for students to check it out from the junior high school.
5 In 2004, the ALA named Judy Blume as the second most censored author in the past 15 years. John Steinbeck was the first.
6 Blume is editor of Places I Never Meant To Be, Original Stories by Censored Writers (Simon & Schuster, 1999).

→ What kind of education is that? It makes me crazy."

The author, who was listed by the US Library of Congress in the living legend category of writers and artists in 2000, also expressed concern about hearing of writers being "dis-invited" from US schools and universities for things they have written or said.

Why do college students need to be warned that what they are about to read might make them feel bad?

"This can be over one incident in a 400-page book," she said. "I thought the idea of education was to exchange ideas and discuss. How we learn from one another?" Nonetheless, she's optimistic that this fearful attitude can be fought against. She has already seen professors and teachers standing up to it.

One thing Blume adamantly doesn't want to see is a return to 1980s America, which was the worse period she has witnessed for freedom to read, and when controversial books were stripped out of classrooms. She believes there has been a return from the precipice of the Reagan era, yet there are still attempts to exert too much control. She referred, very enthusiastically, to The Absolutely True Diary of a Part-Time Indian by Sherman Alexie, which has also caused a stir and was pulled from the curriculum in Idaho schools. What's the problem with it I ask? "The language, the sexuality, all things related to life as a teenage boy. It's like saying it's a bad thing to be a teenage boy!"

"It's the kids' right to read," she said resolutely as our conversation came to a close and she prepared to continue her whirlwind tour. It's a mantra she's been repeating for decades. At 77 and still as dynamic as ever, she shows no sign of stopping anytime soon. ⊗

***Vicky Baker** is deputy editor of Index on Censorship magazine*

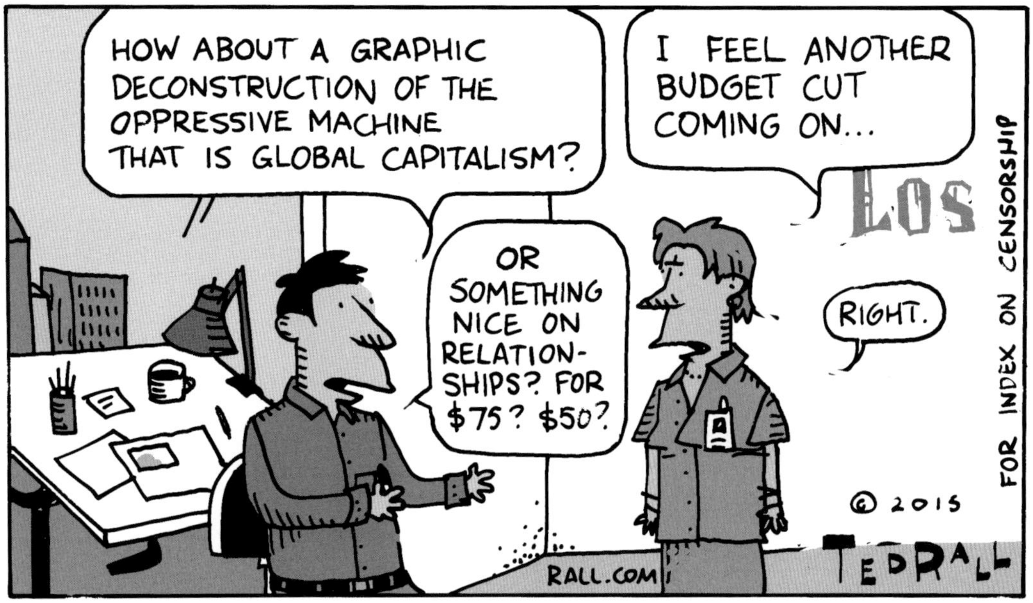

BACKGROUND: Ted Rall was fired from his job as the editorial cartoonist at The Los Angeles Times this summer over a blog-post critical of the LA police. The Association of American Editorial Cartoonists is calling for an independent investigation of the facts and the dismissal–

Drawing down

44(03): 67 | DOI: 10.1177/0306422015605720

Former LA Times contributor **Ted Rall** on why US cartoonists are being forced to play it safe to keep their shrinking pay cheques

CARTOONISTS IN THE US – and, indeed, in many parts of the world – are under pressure to conform to what are increasingly ossified, corporate and slavish media demands.

Cartooning goes back to ancient wall graffiti, but professional cartoonists are subject to the whims of the capitalist system: you have to get paid something to live and breathe current events, politics and culture enough to be able to draw decent cartoons day after day, year after year. As long as I've been in the game, since the late 1980s, it's been a buyer's market. Cartoonists are plentiful, outlets are scarce, so cartoonist salaries (what salaries? no one gets hired full-time anymore), or rather rates, keep dropping. In 1990, I could have gotten $1000 or more per cartoon from a paper like The Los Angeles Times. In 2009, I started at $400. A couple of years later, it was $200.

In a buyer's market, vendors do what they're told. They jump through hoops. They accept censorship. They self-censor. They don't dare to stretch, much less take political or even aesthetic risks. You're lucky to have a gig, they tell you – and they're right.

So cartoons get blander and safer. Which creates a not-so-delicious irony: as the media gets more boring, it loses readers. Which means less money for cartoons. And more pressure on cartoonists to play it safe.

0800 028 8585
REVERSE
NO SMOKING

Under the radar

44(03): 68/71 | DOI: 10.1177/0306422015605721

Security agencies' invasions of privacy are beaten back by public pressure and innovation when they go too far, says **Jamie Bartlett**

THE ARGUMENT OVER national security and individual privacy is certainly a pressing issue, but it's not a new one. How any democratic society weighs up and trades liberty against safety gets re-examined each time a new technology or threat disrupts the established order. Governments have a tendency to see each new technology as a means to help them maintain order; radicals as a way to disrupt it. If governments overreach whatever finely balanced consensus that has been reached on the extent to which governments can monitor its people, there is always a counter-reaction.

To understand the current messy debate about encryption, privacy and terrorism, the best place to start is not with Edward Snowden. One of the first major spy scandals of the modern age took place in 1844 when the British Home Secretary, Sir James Graham, decided to secretly monitor the letters of Giuseppe Mazzini, the exiled leader of La Giovine Italia (Young Italy), a radical movement hoping to create a united Italy. The public and chattering classes of the day rallied against what was largely seen as an indecent breach of individual privacy. This "Post Office Espionage Scandal" more or less put an end to the political spying on letters for 50 years.

Fast forward to the early 1990s, when networked computing was just taking off. Millions logged on for the first time, and, predictably, brought nasty baggage with them. Although still tiny, "cyberspace" was a nuisance to the law. Untraceable paedophile networks were sharing illegal images of children via the net. Anonymous hackers were stealing intellectual property. Internet trolling was rife (although less mean than its modern incarnation).

This made the authorities worried. In the USA, the Federal Bureau of Investigation upped its monitoring of the online world. In 1990, it launched Operation Sun Devil, a nationwide – and over the top – crackdown on hackers. Most importantly, law-makers tried to pass legislation to force telecommunications companies to hand over its customers' details, and prevent the spread of powerful cryptography software. Their arguments were very similar to those of today: they greatly feared a degradation of capability, of the internet going dark, of the terrorists being untraceable, of cyberspace becoming lawless.

But, just as in Mazzini's day, the response was not exactly what the government hoped for. Crime continued, and net users reacted angrily to what they saw as a blatant infringement of civil liberties in this new space. Their space. Leading the counter-attack were the "cypherpunks", a group of Californian libertarians determined to develop and share tools and techniques to keep activity online secret, and to keep the net free of state interference. They set up an email list and ended up predicting, inventing or refining →

LEFT: The Government Communications Headquarters (GCHQ), as portrayed by street artist Banksy, near the agency's base in Cheltenham, UK

Credit: Lamentables/Creative Commons

RIGHT: An abandoned room at the former NSA listening station in Berlin

© Pawel Kopczynski / Reuters

→ almost every technique now employed by computer users to avoid government surveillance. (Julian Assange, posting as "Proff", became a member in 1995.)

It was around this time that a programmer named Phil Zimmerman (although not himself a cypherpunk), who felt alarmed at what to him was a concerted and disproportionate push by the law into citizens' private space, decided to make the code of his "Pretty Good Privacy" software freely available to all. PGP is now an industry standard. Around the same time, the Electronics Frontier Foundation – a digital liberties group – was set up and remains an influential and fierce defender of online privacy.

These struggles were known as the crypto-wars, and they're back. We now share inordinate amounts of information about ourselves online: our bank details, our love life, our holiday snaps; our whole lives are online. More and more of us worry about the digital traces we leave behind: about governments who can monitor what we do; about big tech companies that collect all our data in large centralised servers and sell it; and about invisible US-based regulators exercising control over what happens on the net. The Snowden revelations have turbocharged this movement. But it's about a lot more than intelligence agencies. It's about privacy, freedom, and control.

If we stay vigilant, each time, the balance will tip slightly closer towards greater individual freedom and liberty

Just as in the 1990s, there has been a response – and, again, one which is starting to haunt the companies and intelligence agencies that are perceived to have overreached. Internet privacy and surveillance are now a major political preoccupation. Anonymous browsers, such as Tor, which are used to browse the net without giving away your location, are becoming ever-more popular. Facebook users, who used to be happy sharing everything with anyone, are inching towards more private settings. Phil Zimmermann's PGP encryption is being downloaded by millions. New social media companies and messenger services are popping up with more security built-in.

Motivated by an honourable desire to protect online freedom and privacy, hundreds of computer scientists and internet specialists are working on ingenious ways of keeping online secrets, preventing censorship, and fighting back against centralised control. There will soon be a new generation of easy-to-use auto-encryption email services, such as Mailpile and Dark Mail. Then there are projects like Ethereum, which is building a new web out of the spare power and hard-drive space of millions of connected computers that its owners put on the network. Because it runs with strong encryption and the network is "distributed" across all those individual computers, it's more or less impossible for anyone to censor or control what's on it. Another is called MaidSafe, based in Scotland, which works to similar

principles. Another is Twister. And on, and on. More and more of us – ordinary, typical users – will start using these sorts of systems, because of the obvious benefits.

The upshot is precisely the opposite of what big companies and intelligence agencies want. We're entering into an era where censorship becomes harder and privacy easier. That means more privacy from dictatorships, advertisers, spies, cookies, and hackers. A great development if you care about individual freedom and democracy. But it's also good news if you want to browse child pornography or push out radical Islamist propaganda – both of which benefit from the use of encrypted systems, of course.

The lesson of the 1990s (and the 1840s) is that, in the end, overreaching into the sphere of the individual tends to backfire. But the other lesson is, naturally enough, that spying will not, and cannot, stop (nor should it). The original crypto-war was won by the cypherpunks. Powerful encryption was then de-criminalised in the US, and the attempts to control internet encryption were dropped. But, in response, the NSA and others simply changed tack – and developed ever more sophisticated systems of spying, some of which would eventually turn into the subject of Edward Snowden's revelations.

So spying work will continue – and we desperately need a strong and publicly supported intelligence architecture to help keep us safe: from cyber espionage, terrorism, nuclear proliferation and dictatorial regimes unconstrained by democratic controls. But in a post-Snowden world, the intelligence agencies will have to change the way they work again – becoming more rather than less open. It will have to change its focus: far less mass surveillance, and far more gathering of detailed and careful human intelligence online, more targeted hacking attacks on individuals' devices.

At some point they will overreach once more, and the whole thing will start again. In some ways this is quite a healthy tension for societies that wish to be free and safe. And if we stay vigilant, each time, the balance will tip slightly closer towards greater individual freedom and liberty. ⊗

***Jamie Bartlett** is author of The Dark Net (William Heinemann, 2014) and the director of the Centre for the Analysis of Social Media at the think tank Demos*

Mythbusters

44(03): 72/75 | DOI: 10.1177/0306422015605722

Mark Frary takes a trip through technological secrets and lies to debunk some widely held misconceptions and show which devices, programs and apps you can trust. Illustrations by **Ben Tallon**

HOW DIFFICULT IS it to keep communications secure? If the former CIA employee Edward Snowden's revelations are anything to go by, the answer is almost impossible. But in a world where states are clamping down on the freedom to communicate secretly, we need to know if there are ways to retain privacy.

1. Google listens to your every word

One of Google's coolest features is its voice search but rather creepily you can activate it just by saying "OK Google" to your device. Does this mean it is permanently listening? In fact, you need to have enabled voice detection in Google's settings for this to work. It is enabled when there is a filled-in microphone icon at the right end of the search box and it constantly listens out for you saying OK Google. If you are signed into your Google account, a short audio clip is saved. You can see what they have on you – and delete it – at history.google.com/history/audio. Other devices, such as smart TVs and Xboxes, have similar voice features but these need to be enabled to work. However, many use third-party voice recognition software providers to interpret commands and what you say will be transmitted to those companies.

2. Your phone is tracking you

Yes, it is. Mobile networks can locate you easily by measuring the relative strengths of the signals received from your device by nearby masts using a technique called triangulation. The issue is that the networks also record this information, as was revealed from a freedom of information request by a German Green party member called Malte Spitz. German weekly newspaper Die Zeit turned the information Spitz received from the German telecommunications company Deutsche Telekom into an interactive map which showed him clearly driving along roads, taking public transport and walking along streets.

It is not only networks but also devices which record your movements. Apple's iPhone includes a feature called frequent locations that tracks "places you have recently been, as well as how often and when you visited them, in order to learn places that are significant to you".

It can quickly identify your home and workplace from the amount of time you spend at them and when. Apple says it is used to provide personalised services and is only held on the phone itself. You have to turn it on before it can track you, and to turn it off you need to go into Settings > Privacy > Location services > System service.

3. A Faraday cage will secure my phone

When Edward Snowden was in Hong Kong, he famously asked visitors to place their →

Credit: Ben Tallon

Eggs.
free range

→ phones in the fridge. The idea was that the fridge would act as a Faraday cage, a closed grid of metal blocking radio signals, but this only works from the point the phone is placed in your fridge (and it may well be leaky and not work well). As we saw above, the networks can still track the phone until it disappears into the fridge, and when it reappears. So the tracker would be able to have a good guess at where you are. The desire to have secure mobile comms has led to the development of the Blackphone, a new enterprise-level device from Swiss company Silent Circle, which runs on a custom version of Android called Silent OS and encrypts voice, video and texts on the device as standard.

4. Air gaps make computers secure

High-security operations, such as the military or nuclear installations, often use air-gapped computers – ones that are not connected to any external networks, particularly the internet – to improve security. The idea is that the computer cannot get infected by malware or other viruses since the computer can only receive data and files through USB sticks or being hardwired to other computers on the network. However, in 2010, it was revealed that USB sticks had been used to infect air-gapped computers in nuclear installations in Iran with the Stuxnet worm.

The desire to have secure communications has led to the development of the Blackphone, which encrypts voice, video and texts as standard

More recently, researchers at Ben Gurion University in Israel have demonstrated a proof of concept for a technique known as AirHopper, which allowed them to gain access to an air-gapped computer through a nearby mobile phone by intercepting radio waves from the monitor.

5. Your laptop camera is spying on you

Possibly. Programmes usually have to ask for explicit permission to use the webcam or microphone on your computer and this is the default setting. However, certain types of malware target this permission dialogue and can bypass the permission request, as Miss Teen USA 2013, Cassidy Wolf, found to her horror when a stalker secretly took naked pictures of her at home by hacking her computer and activating the webcam. The surest way to protect against such attacks is perhaps the lowest tech – stick a piece of tape over your camera until you need to use it.

6. Using a virtual private network (VPN) makes communication secure

Dissidents and others who want to access banned websites or forums often use VPNs to get around obstacles such as the Chinese firewall.

A VPN – a means of sending data securely across public networks – is a little like an undersea tunnel: it connects the two ends and traffic can pass along it without anyone along the route being able to see what is being transmitted. Any attempt to break into the tunnel is futile as it gets flooded. Another advantage of a VPN is that many offer the possibility of being anonymous.

VPNs rely on a number of techniques to stay secure. Client software on your local device and software at the server are authenticated while data passing through the VPN is encrypted by the sender and decrypted by the receiver. Transmissions also often include measures to ensure integrity which will reveal if the data has been intercepted in transmission.

So can you really remain anonymous? Some VPNs that promise anonymous access also show in their small-print terms that they log any activity that you get up to while connected through their service. Of those that claim not to log activity, many would reveal information about their users if served with a valid court order. Some also doubt that providers who claim they do not log activity are not being secretly monitored by security agencies.

7. Encryption systems like the Pretty Good Privacy (PGP) work

Most of the encryption techniques used today to keep communications secure rely on asymmetric cryptography, a system that uses two keys – essentially numbers – which are mathematically related to encrypt and decrypt information. The popular email encryption system PGP uses asymmetric cryptography as one of its encryption steps, while the technique is also at the heart of the RSA security system used by many companies.

The security of such systems lies in the mathematics. In the case of RSA, the security comes from the fact that it is easy to multiply two large prime numbers together to work out their product but fiendishly difficult to work out the two original numbers from the answer. Early versions of such systems have been compromised as computing power to work out the answer by brute force has become cheaper and faster.

The worry has been that security organisations like the US National Security Agency have worked out shortcuts to these mathematical problems. Snowden's revelations appear to confirm that properly implemented encryption systems can still keep traffic secret but that the NSA exploits vulnerabilities elsewhere.

Highly secure technologies do exist but, as governments get more interested in what their citizens are doing, demand for technology to help keep the communications of dissidents, journalists and others with a need for privacy is rising. However, what Edward Snowden has made abundantly clear is that even if perfect technology exists, there are many weak links that can be exploited – vulnerable individuals and compliant and complicity corporates who routinely hand over details of what has passed over their networks. In light of this, is it perhaps time to ditch the technology and go back to the old-fashioned methods of secret communication? Invisible ink anyone? ⊗

© *Mary Frary*

Mark Frary *worked as a researcher at the CERN laboratory in Geneva. He now writes regularly for The Times newspaper and is the author of eight books including Codebreaker: The History of Secret Communication*

Credit: Darley Shen/ Reuters

Clearing the air: investigating Weibo censorship in China

44(03): 76/79 | DOI: 10.1177/0306422015605724

When a documentary about air pollution in China went viral, the Chinese government first welcomed it, then tried to have it removed. In this new research, academics **Matthew Auer** and **King-wa Fu** reveal how they monitored the takedown of microbloggers' comments

LEFT: Air pollution in China's Hubei province, pictured on 6 March 2015, the day of the annual meeting of parliament and week after the Under the Dome documentary was released

CHAI JING'S TONE was part dispassionate science, part outrage. A former reporter for state-owned broadcaster China Central Television, she was fronting Under the Dome, a documentary that methodically explains the lethal hazards of microscopic, airborne soot in cities across China. She also spoke plainly about her concerns for her daughter's health. Especially moving was a video interview featuring a six-year-old girl's testimony to having never seen white clouds, stars, or blue skies.

The film rapidly went viral. Public interest in the documentary's primary villain, "haze" (or smog), surged. On Monday 2 March this year, around 48 hours after its online release, the 104-minute documentary had been viewed more than 200 million times and references to haze appeared in more than 280 million posts on Weibo, China's equivalent of Twitter. We found that hundreds of posts were censored in the hours and days after the video was first uploaded to the web.

Using selective sampling technology developed by the Weiboscope project at the University of Hong Kong (see sidebar), we monitored Weibo posts related to Under the Dome. While news of the documentary caught the attention of the international media, censorship of Weibo has not yet been revealed. Among the deleted messages we found condemnations of the state and photographs of anti-pollution demonstrations.

This was an abrupt turnaround. The website of the People's Daily had been one of the first platforms to make Under the Dome available, and hence, an important media organ of the Chinese Communist Party assented to its distribution. Early on, the video and Chai gained praise from China's minister of the environment. But official endorsements were quickly offset by stern warnings from national and municipal authorities that media coverage of Under the Dome should cease. When links to the video went dead and commentary was pulled down from outlets, including the People's Daily, news outlets around the world took notice.

What they missed was that hundreds of posts were censored on 1 and 2 March, days before the video started disappearing from popular video-sharing sites, such as Youku and Tencent. Among the deleted messages were condemnations of a key assertion in the video – that China's dirty air was a "collective sin", a public health crisis perpetrated by China's rank and file. "Blaming it on the powerless citizens is simply ignorant and shameless," declared the author of a censored post. Other censored messages criticised the state-owned oil and gas corporation, Sinopec, or poked fun at recent emergency measures to scrub Beijing's air in time for a meeting of the Asia-Pacific Economic Cooperation forum – a fleeting, fair-weather event that gave rise to the ironic phrase, "APEC Blue". →

Among censored posts were images of demonstrators. To our knowledge, public demonstrations in response to the documentary have not been described elsewhere, and while we cannot vouch for the authenticity of the images, it is notable that censors felt compelled to take them down. One censored image, which was accompanied by text, purportedly showed demonstrators in the eastern city of Xi'an carrying signs, reading "Haze causes cancer, harming everyone" and "To control haze, the government should take responsibility".

Among the deleted messages were condemnations of a key assertion in the video – that China's dirty air was a "collective sin"

In China, exhortations on online forums, blogs, and microblogs calling for people to collectively object to government actions or policies are all but certain to provoke censors. As Professor Gary King, director of the Institute for Quantitative Social Science at Harvard University, has argued, censors get to work when posted information is interpreted as inciting collective action (How Censorship In China Allows Government Criticism But Silences Collective Expression, in American Political Science Review, May 2013). However, King also contended in the same article that ordinary expressions of dissent online, even bitter criticisms of government policy, are now regularly tolerated. Yet the censored Weibo posts we compiled indicate that public expressions of concern, well short of pleas for a collective response, were deemed worrisome enough by authorities to be suppressed. Blocked messages linked to Under the Dome included many jabs at ineffective regulatory policies and sarcastic assessments of gov-

Examples of censored Weibo posts

1 MARCH 2015
Ever since the first day of policy ban, the worst we fear in this country was never the haze, but restless evil hands hiding behind the haze!

1 MARCH 2015
I agree with this statement from Murong Xuecun: The emergence of haze is not attributed to the lack of supervision from government but the lack of supervision on government.

3 MARCH 2015
Just saw these words: "Haze is a collective sin, it is worsening China's overall environment, and all of us are conspirators." I strongly disagree with the statement. Let me spell out the words that were implied in Chai Jing's film: No matter how complicated the reason for the polluted haze is, it's our system's fault at the end of the day. The authorities know the source of haze, and quickly reacted, created APEC blue, this is plain and simple for everyone to see. Blaming it on the powerless citizens is simply ignorant and shameless.

5 MARCH 2015
Care for pneumoconiosis in China! You can know the disaster brought by haze! Country needs development, but what we need more is public health!// @What is law:// Lawyer [name redacted]: The number of retweets, comments and likes of this post have exceeded ten thousand, with the number of reading amounting 3.05 million.

8 MARCH 2015
To deal with haze problem, the government should undertake the responsibility.

ernment performance, but neither explicit nor implicit calls for collective action (see sidebar). Notable exceptions were images of placard-carrying demonstrators. By the standards of Chinese censors, the messages conveyed by the protesters are not the problem. It is that they are demonstrating in the first place.

Chinese as well as Western media outlets report that President Xi Jinping is serious about cleaning up pollution and in engaging the public on this issue. In the tradition of Chinese mass mobilisation, which sees campaigns involving matters as diverse as fighting corruption and planting trees to curb erosion, President Xi has appealed to "the whole society" to "act more vigorously to protect the land our lives depend on". Broad, public participation is required to rectify a collective sin, according to Under the Dome, which has been compared to Rachel Carson's book Silent Spring in bringing environmental damage to public attention. Successful environmental policies in industrialising nations often involve putting public pressure on governmental authorities to act, not merely to exhort public participation and promising to punish violators – both of which are already typical in Chinese environmental policy.

The brief, but widespread, availability of the documentary Under the Dome underscores Chinese authorities' ambivalence towards a more proactive approach to the country's environmental crisis. The panicky removal of the video from Chinese websites, followed by censorship of not only official commentary, but also the views of ordinary citizens, suggests that the state remains more effective at clamping down on public expression than on pollution.

Additional reporting: Xinle Jia, Priscilla Lee and William Ash

Matthew R. Auer *is a professor of environmental studies and dean of the faculty at Bates College, USA. His recent research considers public understanding of environmental issues in China as revealed in microblogging activity.*

King-wa Fu *is an associate professor at the Journalism and Media Studies Centre of the University of Hong Kong. His research interests include internet censorship and computational social sciences*

PERMISSION DENIED!

How we tracked censorship on Weibo

Weibo, like most web services, uses an application programming interface (API) to enable posts to be accessed by a variety of screens and software, including websites and mobile devices. It allows access to each and every post on Weibo, including the content of the post accompanied by metadata, such as the date, time, name of user etc. The Weiboscope project at the University of Hong Kong makes use of this API to track microblogging activity and all associated content from a list of around 350,000 popular Weibo users who have 1,000 or more followers.

We collected user posts on 1 March and 2 March this year. Using the "user timeline" function of the API, all posts were saved in a PostgreSQL database. The script we developed scours the posting activity, hourly and daily, to detect deleted messages, including censored messages, which generate a particular error code. The code for each deleted post is accompanied with a "Permission Denied!" message. Extrapolating from a sample of censored posts, we estimate, conservatively, that hundreds of posts were censored during this time period.

NGOs: under fire, under surveillance

44(03): 80/82 | DOI: 10.1177/0306422015605727

After assassinations and break-ins, what lies ahead for South Africa's campaigners? Amid fears of restrictive new legislation, **Natasha Joseph** looks at the pitfalls of scrutinising a changeable country

CIVIL SOCIETY ORGANISATIONS and workers' unions in South Africa are operating in a climate of fear and suspicion amid growing evidence that the government's State Security Agency is monitoring their members. They are also uneasily watching the country's parliament amid suggestions that the legislation governing non-profit organisations may change radically in the coming years. There have been similar legislative changes in Russia and, closer to home, in Uganda, Malawi and Zambia, which have seriously hampered the ability of these organisations to operate.

The attitudes of the governing African National Congress towards the civil society sector have changed several times in the two decades since apartheid ended. Currently, says Section27's executive director Mark Heywood, "there is no uniform view in government" about whether organisations are friend or foe. Section27 is a public interest law centre that litigates around social justice issues like access to housing, education and sanitation. It incorporates one of the country's most famous NGOs, the Aids Law Project, which in the early 2000s went to court to force the government to provide treatment preventing the transmission of HIV from pregnant mothers to their unborn children.

It won, the victory coming at the height of then-President Thabo Mbeki's era of Aids denialism. Heywood was an integral part of that campaign, which was run in the courts by the Aids Law Project and on the streets by the Treatment Action Campaign. He told Index on Censorship that there was "more trust in government among ordinary South Africans" at that time and the organisations' work was seen by some ANC members and supporters as being tantamount to treason.

The judgment was a turning point for many people's attitudes to civil society organisations and NGOs, and today South Africa boasts what many worldwide consider a model approach to HIV treatment programmes. On the flipside, the government is viewed with increasing dissatisfaction and mistrust as it seeks to provide healthcare, housing, sanitation, education, a stable supply of electricity and job opportunities to its citizens while battling economic uncertainty.

Heywood said that while there were those in government who "would like to work more openly and constructively with us"; there are others who resent "the echo that we're creating". Civil society organisations, including Section27 and the anti-censorship campaign group Right2Know, ask difficult questions, putting a spotlight on government failings and, in Section27's case, using the country's powerful constitution and its well-regarded courts to hold the government to account on its social responsibilities.

"The securocrats in government view us as an enemy," Heywood said. There's a view that, since President Jacob Zuma took office in 2009, the securocrats have become increasingly powerful and have captured a number of crucial state organisations – including the State Security Agency, the priority crimes division of the police service, and the tax collection agency.

Those in power who want to sideline civil society accuse it of being funded by nefarious

Several NGOs have reported break-ins at their offices during which only computer hard drives are taken and valuables are left untouched

Western interests that want to return South Africa to white rule. Recently, the Southern African Litigation Centre was criticised by the government for its role in trying to obtain an arrest warrant for Sudanese leader Omar al-Bashir while he was in the country for an African Union summit. The centre was accused of behaving in an anti-African →

OPPOSITE: Members of South African housing rights group Abahlali baseMjondolo at a protest in Durban. Several of their members have been assassinated and the organisers believe the unknown perpetrators wanted to shutdown the call for proper housing

Credit: Inkani~commonswiki/ Creative Commons

→ fashion by taking on one of the continent's own leaders.

Heywood said attempts by those in power to stigmatise the sector have been largely unsuccessful: "We've not encountered any hostility in the communities where we work and help. The people who buy that type of nonsense are not ordinary people."

"The stigma strategy doesn't work as well as it used to, so [their methods of countering us] become more insidious," he explained. For instance, several NGOs have reported break-ins at their offices during which only computer hard drives are taken and valuables are left untouched. These kinds of incidents, Heywood said, are supposed to intimidate workers – a way of saying "we can get you".

These organisations are getting too close to revealing an individual or group's involvement in corruption. Bullets guarantee silence

There have also been less subtle incidents. In a report entitled Big Brother Exposed, Right2Know shared stories from community and civil society activists who say they have been followed by state security agents and had their phone conversations recorded. The government has denied these allegations.

Most worryingly, some activists have died because of their work. The Durban-based housing rights group Abahlali basMjondolo said several of its members have been assassinated by those wanting to shut down the fight for proper housing. Heywood said smaller organisations with less sophisticated structures and fewer support networks were far more vulnerable to this kind of violence than their counterparts at bigger, more established organisations.

Why would anyone resort to murder to shut down a protester or social movement? Because, in many cases, these organisations are getting too close to revealing an individual or group's involvement in corruption, Heywood said. In the case of an organisation like Abahlali baseMjondolo, which tries to lift communities out of shacks and into formal housing, they may be interfering with someone's access to a lucrative government tender. Bullets guarantee silence.

There's plenty for civil society in South Africa to celebrate. Heywood said the sector had the ability to litigate, access to a strong and vibrant media (still one of the most free in Africa) and, of course, the cornerstone of modern South Africa, its constitution. "Civil society is getting stronger again, and organisations are learning from and becoming more engaged with each other," said Heywood.

With local government elections scheduled for next year, it remains to be seen whether the situation will worsen for these organisations or if government attitudes will change for the better, fostering the dissent and transparency every country needs. ⊗

***Natasha Joseph** is a contributing editor to Index on Censorship and education editor of The Conversation Africa. She is based in Cape Town*

"Some words are more powerful than guns"

44(03): 83/85 | DOI: 10.1177/0306422015605731

Gene Sharp has spent six decades promoting non-violent struggle against authoritarian regimes, bringing him jail time, Nobel Peace Prize nominations and the ire of dictators across the world. **Alan Leo** talks to him about the power of words, his contact with Albert Einstein, and why Angola is the latest regime to fear his works

ANGOLAN SECURITY FORCES burst into a home in its capital city Luanda at the end of June and detained 13 young men – "caught red-handed" in the words of Angola's interior ministry. The offence? Meeting to discuss books about non-violent democratic reform, including From Dictatorship to Democracy, a tract on non-violent struggle by US political theorist Gene Sharp.

Amid a widening crackdown against critics of Angolan president José Eduardo dos Santos and his 36-year authoritarian rule, the jailing of a book club struck observers as a particularly naked assault on free expression. "The Angolan regime is afraid of books," wrote Angolan journalist and Index on Censorship award winner Rafael Marques de Morais. But why?

Index put the question to Sharp, whose works – which also include Sharp's Dictionary of Power and Struggle and his three-volume opus, The Politics of Nonviolent Action – have been suppressed by authoritarian regimes around the world, from Burma to Belarus, Iran and China.

"They have good reason to be afraid," said Sharp. "Some words are more powerful than guns."

Political power, in Sharp's view, is never taken; it is only given by the people. From Dictatorship suggests 198 ways people can stop giving.

That idea has animated 87-year-old Sharp for six decades, from his own imprisonment for civil disobedience in the 1950s, through an academic career researching theories of non-violent struggle, to his establishment in 1983 of the Albert Einstein Institution, which supports research and education to translate those theories into action around the world.

Einstein wrote the introduction to Sharp's first book, a study of Mahatma Gandhi's non-violent tactics. The young Sharp, facing prosecution for civil disobedience in his stance against US conscription during →

ABOVE: Gene Sharp pictured in in his office in Boston in 2009

→ the Korean conflict, had written to the eminent scholar and pacifist seeking advice – and a favour.

"He supported people who were standing up for free speech, and who were in trouble because of that," Sharp said. Einstein had his work blacklisted in Nazi Germany, was targeted under McCarthyism when he moved to the US, and spoke up for human rights throughout his career. "So I wrote him a letter and said, 'Excuse me, but I'm about to go to jail. And by the way, I have this manuscript of a book on how Gandhi used civil disobedience and non-violent struggle.'"

To Sharp's surprise, Einstein agreed to write the introduction and the two continued their correspondence until Sharp went to prison. The book, with Einstein's introduction, was not published until after the physicist's death.

"I never met him," said Sharp, who is nominated for the Nobel Peace Prize for the fourth time this year. "I should have, I guess. The executor of his estate, Otto Nathan, scolded me later for not going down to Princeton. But I was also getting ready to go to jail."

Today, Sharp believes his understanding of Gandhi was in some ways naive. Like others, Sharp thought that Gandhi's followers converted some opponents through the moral weight of their non-violent tactics. "I believed you could melt their hearts," said Sharp, palms pressed in supplication below sarcastic puppy-dog eyes.

The classic example was Gandhi's first campaign of mass civil disobedience, against caste-based segregation in the Indian village of Vykom. Sharp said he now agrees with political scientist Mary King, whose recent book Gandhian Nonviolent Struggle and Untouchability in South India argues that the Vaikom Satyagraha, as this practice of resistance was known, did not melt the hearts of the upper castes; small concessions were instead squeezed from the state through tactical pressure and compromise.

The tactical, rather than moral, dimensions of non-violent struggle have defined Sharp's later work. Sharp said he disdains violence not as a pacifist but as a strategist. "The idea that power comes out of the barrel of a gun," he said, "was an idiotic statement from someone who didn't know anything about how to win a revolution."

In 1993, Burmese dissident U Tin Maung Win asked Sharp to contribute to his underground journal, New Era. Sharp told Tin Maung Win he was unfamiliar with Burma but offered to write in general terms about strategic non-violence. The result was From Dictatorship to Democracy, which has since been translated into more than 40 languages and praised by democracy activists from Serbia to Indonesia to Ukraine to the Arab Spring.

Sharp's influence has led critics from authoritarian regimes and the far left to accuse him of fomenting "soft coups" on behalf of the US government. In response, 138 scholars and activists, including Noam Chomsky and Howard Zinn, signed a 2008 letter supporting Sharp and rejecting any link between the Albert Einstein Institution and US foreign policy.

Sharp is used to suspicion. Soviet agents trailed him through the Baltic states in 1991, Chinese agents outside Tiananmen Square in 1989. "They were quite friendly," he recalled. "Spoke excellent English. 'Who are you? What are you doing here? And so forth."

The Albert Einstein Institution does not seek out activists, Sharp said, and it offers its materials to anyone who asks. In a statement expressing concern about the detention of Sharp's readers in Angola, the institution offered its resources to Angola's president. If Dos Santos is truly worried about a coup, the statement read, "We recommend that he read our publication, The Anti-Coup, on how non-violent action can deter and defeat coups d'état."

In recent years, the institution has operated out of Sharp's home in East Boston, a working-class neighbourhood of immigrants adjacent to Logan airport. The comfortable, shabby offices befit a retired academic, but Sharp has no interest in retirement. He and

His book, which was originally smuggled into Burma by river, can now be downloaded from anywhere in the world

the institute's five-person staff are working hard to collect, revise and publish six decades of work, driven by an unspoken urgency to keep up all the work while Sharp still has the energy.

The institution's website offers most of Sharp's works for free. From Dictatorship to Democracy, which was originally smuggled into Burma by river, can now be downloaded from anywhere in the world. In the last year, they say the site has tallied visits from all but four countries.

"This new technology is much more dangerous," Sharp said. And dictators know it.

"The regimes have become more aware of my writing," he said. "Maybe≠ because I became more explicit about how you can get rid of these regimes, the fact they're not permanent, they don't last forever. They're on their way out.

"And they don't like news like that." ⊗

__Alan Leo__ is a journalist based in Boston, Massachusetts. More on the Albert Einstein Institution can be found at aeinstein.org. The winner of the Nobel Peace Prize will be announced on 9 October 2015

Taking back the web

44(03): 86/88 | DOI: 10.1177/0306422015605732

Can users take back the internet to evade heavy control from state censors and corporations? **Jason DaPonte** looks at technology companies putting free expression first as they launch new apps and communication systems

"**CENSORSHIP HAS ONLY** ramped up and become more widespread, and now even circumvention tools are being disrupted. The situation is much worse than 10 years ago," said the founder of GreatFire, a technological activist group helping to get content to Chinese citizens, speaking to Index on condition of anonymity.

Technology has allowed users to circumvent internet censorship for many years, but it has often been a complicated process for regular users. Now, a new generation is emerging, with a focus on decentralisation, open sourcing and easy-to-use encryption.

Among them is GreatFire's FreeBrowser mobile application, which currently has more than nine million users and is already providing significant access to content that the Chinese government has blocked or deleted. It looks no different from a typical mobile web browser but it gets to uncensored internet content by directing Chinese users through complex paths on the internet, which are difficult to block. No complex systems or virtual private networks (VPNs) are needed.

GreatFire uses its website to monitor sites being blocked in China, and runs FreeWeibo, which hosts content deleted by censors from Weibo, a Chinese microblogging site (similar to Twitter). The two sites have nearly 16 million users, but progress is still hard and they said that new technological threats are always emerging.

The group describes its approach as "collateral freedom" – think the opposite of collateral damage – and takes advantage of the fact that more than half of the web's traffic is delivered via content delivery networks. CDNs are made up of dispersed servers that allow content from multiple owners to be distributed across the internet. "In order for the authorities to block content they disapprove of, they would have to block access to all CDNs. But they will not do this because there would be significant economic fallout from cutting China off from half of the world's internet," said GreatFire's founder.

The New York-based technology start-up Minds gives users free access to content by creating a social network that feels familiar to anyone who has used Facebook, Twitter or any of the other leading social platforms. The difference is that it has an open-source codebase and an encrypted private messenger, which means that the rules by which it shows content will be governed by its community and its private messages will be almost impossible to intercept.

It sprang to notoriety in the spring when its launch was "backed" by some of the activist groups called Anonymous.

"The encryption is foundational but we're having success because you don't have to install complicated stuff – it's just like signing up for other social networks," Minds founder Bill Ottman told Index. One of the company's goals is to bring open-source and encrypted technology to the masses, he said.

Instead of holding complete control over its codebase and user data, Minds makes it freely available worldwide, allowing developers to work on the code. This improves the core product and ensures transparency: the algorithms that display content aren't centrally controlled and the community can determine how they work (rather than their being tuned to maximise advertising revenue or potentially block content). "Our 'boost' functionality is an ad network that doesn't spy on people," Ottman said.

Minds is commercially and technically federating with other major open-source players and is backing a movement called the "internet migration".

"The 'internet migration' is all about migrating the internet to open-source encrypted platforms. Every time you create an account on an encrypted service, choose to use Firefox (open source) instead of Chrome (privately held by Google), these are the micro moves that help to shift the power structure of the internet," Ottman said. Users are slowly "taking back" the internet as they recognised the need for open-source, transparent tools and encrypted communication.

This autumn, Minds will host encrypted video chat on its platform using peer-to-peer technology, which does not require a central server. It also hopes to eventually create an offshore centre with distributed data, so users can decide where and how their data is held.

Ottman admits that storage is an issue for the company because it uses Amazon Web Services (as do most major websites). While Mind's policy is never to hand over private data, access could still be secured by a government if it compels Amazon to surrender it. Still, with the data encrypted, it would be very difficult for anyone to crack.

Bill Levy, technical director of GCHQ, the UK's surveillance centre, recently spoke at a BT Tower Talk on digital security in London about the type of encryption that Minds →

ABOVE: Technology giant Apple has policies on the type of content that can appear in its iTunes Store, which means start-up companies have to play by its rules or risk limiting their reach. Here, an Apple store in the Chinese city of Hangzhou is prepared for its opening in early 2015

Credit: Reuters/Chance Chan

→ uses. He said: "The best estimate for the number of bits of work to decrypt just one [encrypted] session is 280 [1,208,925,819 ,614,629,174,706,176] and with the best processor we have today requiring 10 nanojoules per instruction, that works out at 3.4 terawatt hours per 50 minutes, which is the entire power generating capacity of the UK … Even if an intelligence agency wants

If an intelligence agency wants to break encryption, it is a great deal more work than anybody realises because laws of physics still apply

to break encryption, it is a great deal more work than anybody realises because the laws of physics still apply."

Minds faces another threat from giant internet corporations because it distributes its mobile apps through Google Play and Apple's iTunes Store. Both have rules about the type of content that can appear and, while no content is filtered on the PC version of the Minds, Ottman said the company was forced to look at what content was promoted on the mobile versions or risk losing the ability to be installed on mobile devices. This bothered him and he hoped to find a way around it. And he said: "Our ultimate policy is: if it's legal, it's OK."

A different route to free access to internet content is offered by Outernet, a satellite-communications company. By making content available to users globally via satellite, it bypasses the internet as a delivery mechanism altogether. Every inhabitable part of the globe is covered by satellite reception, yet around half of the world's population cannot gain access to the internet because of lack of infrastructure.

"What I want to solve is information access – so we send the content down just like TV or radio," Syed Karim, founder and chief executive of Outernet, told Index. His goal was a media company that could reach every person on the planet with ease.

As satellite signals are very difficult to block, this delivery mechanism can get content into regimes that try to control the internet. Just as China faces great difficulty in preventing GreatFire's FreeBrowser getting content from CDNs, blocking satellite signals could create major impacts for any country that tried to do it, because other satellite communications (including in neighbouring countries) could be blocked.

Karim recognises the irony in Outernet's use of the same satellite to deliver its content over China as the Chinese state uses to deliver censored television. He hopes one day the company will have its own satellites, which would remove any threats of being censored by satellite operators.

Outernet aims to create a "library in the sky" of content selected by a global group of community editors and publishers. Users would download the content at up to 100 gigabytes per day, to store on a hard drive and then browse via their PC or mobile device.

The company is offering two devices compatible with its system (one mobile and one fixed), which will download, store and locally serve data. It is also making the plans for creating a receiver publicly available. "As long as you offer a public spec, you don't even have to depend on hardware which may be illegal or difficult to get. So people can build their own receiver, even if they can't buy it," Karim said.

If the "internet migration" catches on, it will bring a new chapter in the struggle for democratic control of the internet, which has maintained what independence it has by being a system that self-corrects when its users mobilise en masse. ⊗

***Jason DaPonte** is the former head of BBC Mobile and founder of The Swarm consultancy*

Credit: Osman Orsal /Reuters

CULTURE

In this section

MAIN: A man searches for a book in a second hand book market in Istanbul

New word (dis)order

44(03): 93/101 | DOI: 10.1177/0306422015605733

Novelist **Kaya Genç** talks to **Rachael Jolley** about his new short story, how it was inspired by the historical moment when his nation's language lost thousands of words and why his government is now introducing Ottoman language classes. All illustrations for the short story, published below, by **Molly Crabapple**

AROUND 90,000 WORDS are estimated to have disappeared from the Turkish language in the 1930s, when Turkish leader Kemal Ataturk decided to get rid of the Arabic script and "Ottoman" words as part of a modernisation plan. At the same time, Ataturk decided to move the Turks to a Latin script, and make written Turkish closer to the language spoken on the streets.

This period of immense upheaval and radical change was the inspiration for a new short story by novelist Kaya Genç, In the Court of Purity, and a set of illustrations by the acclaimed artist Molly Crabapple.

This period of dramatic lingustic change is currently back under discussion, with Ottoman Turkish now being taught again in schools.

Genç said: "I have spent this year studying the subject intensely and when I came across Geoffrey Lewis's book The Turkish Language Reform: A Catastrophic Success, I was fascinated by the history of Turkey's language reform. Lewis gives a hilarious account of all the committees and figures who led the effort of purifying Turkish from what they saw as 'foreign words'."

"Language and script revolutions have done both good and bad: Arabic script absolutely failed to represent Turkish sounds and the change in the script most certainly democratised the literary scene and created a generation of readers fascinated by literature. I think language reform is more problematic: in the hands of Turkish ultra-nationalists the cleansing of language became a very ideological enterprise which cut off writers, like me, from a fascinating literary tradition," he said.

The novelist, whose book Angry Young Turkey is due to be published next year, said: "I think it is an interesting subject for readers today because Turkey seems to have finally reached a maturity and made peace with its Ottoman past and cultural heritage. Leftists are looking at the late Ottoman era to find their ideological ancestors; Kemalists have realised that Ataturk wrote in Arabic script for a long time and learning Arabic script helps them better grasp his vision. The Ministry of Education has opened Ottoman language classes in high schools, so the new generation will probably be able to read Turkish literature in both Ottoman and modern Latin script." →

Illustrations: Molly Crabapple

In the Court of Purity

One day in 1934, a middle-aged man woke up from a terrible nightmare in the crimson-coloured bedroom of an old Istanbul mansion. For what felt like an interminable length of time he dreamt about a dark court of law that was filled with dozens of prisoners who looked at him with an expression of sad desperation in their coal-black eyes. In the dream, he was a Great Judge to whom was given the power to kill or save those sickly men. Prisoners were placed inside large metal cages at the centre of the courtroom. He could see their long, untrimmed beards and yellow faces; their claw-like hands reached out from the cages and their wet palms were visible from the podium where he sat. Their voices, in contrast, were incomprehensible to him – just a murmur filling the room and spiralling out from the cage, spelling out a message that was inaudible but no doubt addressed to him. From behind the group of prisoners, he discerned a figure who eyed him with an intensity that sent shivers down his spine. Dressed in a blindingly bright red uniform, this man moved his hands self-assuredly and was certainly a man of previous, recently lost, authority. He looked at this glowing prisoner in awe and fear and felt, on his shoulders, the responsibility of deciding his fate – whether he should be saved or perish was entirely left to him. But before he could say or do anything, guards appeared in four corners of the courtroom. They approached the cage, entered it, brought the red-coloured prisoner out, placed a piece of cloth around his head and took him away.

Two hours later, in the garden of Istanbul's most lavish building, the Dolmabahçe Palace, the dreamer realised what had terrified him in this nightmare that morning. Without knowing it, he had experienced the moment just after the decision, rather than just before. This had become a recurrent nightmare during the last few years as his responsibilities as a man of letters grew. The dreamer lit a cigarette and heard himself tell Abdülkadir, his dear friend who watched him apparently surprised, the following words: "This has become my biggest fear now. It is terrifying to no longer be able to reverse one's decision."

"My dear Rıfkı," Abdülkadir said. "What is there to be so terribly anxious about? As a writer your most serious life decision is to make up your mind about whether a comma or an apostrophe works better in a sentence. I assure you that those unused apostrophes or exclamation marks are not locked up somewhere; nor will they come after you in the future for revenge. Let's attend this so-called dictionary committee session this morning; afterwards we will have *rakı* in Beyoğlu and laugh at your silly dreams and fears."

They started walking on the narrow gravel road that outstretched to the palace entrance. As he looked at it, Rıfkı realised how the zigzag road resembled a long, elaborate sentence with numerous sub-clauses that complicate it. He saw tiny by-roads that connected the main gravel road to different compartments of the palace – he had often wanted to visit those auxiliary buildings during the two years he had spent here: he heard there were other committees in them responsible for different fields, such as archaeology or biology.

Both Rıfkı and Abdülkadir were perfectly dressed in black trousers and jackets; they both had Oxford shoes; once inside they both took off their hats before raising their heads to look at the image of the Great Leader hung on the wall. As they climbed the marble stairs that led to the hall upstairs, the Leader's eyes followed them. Inside the committee room, where a different-sized version of the same image was hung on the wall, the eyes reappeared and Rıfkı felt safe in their presence.

Rıfkı's closeness to the Great Leader was an open secret, viewed suspiciously by Abdülkadir and his fellow men of letters. In the early 1930s, Rıfkı has worked as a member of the legendary Turkish Society for the Study of Language and was known as a passionate purifier (*tasfiyeci*), a term used for linguists and writers whose job it was to find Turkish substitutes for words with Arabic and Persian etymologies. Purity had become the key concept of this decade: in an effort to cleanse Turkish language from all traces of foreignness, purifiers had started a nation-wide effort to find ethnically pure, Turkic replacements for words suspected of having eastern, Islamic roots.

One reason why people were suspicious of Rıfkı was his role as a frequent guest of the Great Leader's famous drinking parties where he could observe whether words selected by his colleagues went down well with him – he used to report back what he had heard in the morning, "*he loves the new word for soldier but hated the word for* home".

1932 had been a busy year for the purifiers. Among other things they had banned the Arabic call to prayer (*Allahu Ekber!*) in Turkish mosques, replacing it with a Turkish version (*Tanrı uludur!*). Such reforms, they thought, offered the best way of defeating the Ottoman heritage which, they believed, nobody would be interested in looking at from now on. "Turkish is going to be a language as independent and free as the great Turkish nation," the Great Leader told Rıfkı not so long ago, "and with it we will enter the world of civilisation at one go, just like that".

But four days ago, on Thursday, things took a strange turn with the politician abruptly summoning the writer to his palace. There, enveloped in smoke, he seemed very concerned about the purifying business. Many of the words they picked as replacements were strongly disliked by people to whom they were intended to serve, he said.

"We have reached a dead end, Rıfkı. Deleting those words from the language complicates things, rather than simplifying them. People can no longer do commerce on streets... The most basic concepts, like a discount, or a loan, cannot be used simply because people don't know the new words for them. Our public life has been strongly wounded by our experiment, Rıfkı... What we need to do now is to put an end to the purifying business but do so in such a way that nobody will laugh at what we did in the past. We will keep on talking about the purification process while immediately starting a new initiative to →

gayret
kâmus
vilayet
âbide
hüküm

hasilat
müBalağa

save words on your long list from deletion. We will not say, 'we changed our mind and decided to keep Arabic and Persian words in the language...' No, Rıfkı! We will say, 'we are keeping those words because they are actually Turkish!'"

To this Rıfkı replied with what had seemed to him like the most obvious question one could think of. "But, Great Leader, how can we tell people that an Arabic or Persian word is in fact Turkish? It would be like trying to prove that a monkey is in fact a donkey!"

Rıfkı remembered his daring words as the Committee Leader took his seat on the podium. This tall man then started eyeing the room where anxious linguists were getting ready to voice their defences for words suspected of impurity. On Friday Rıfkı had sent committee members letters about the new line about old-fashioned words – informing them that they would be saved, instead of purged from language from now on – and this must have led to a sense of unease among them judging from the anxious complexions of the men filling the room. The Committee Leader (his literature professor at college; a man he thoroughly respected) was the only person to whom he did not send a copy of the letter because Rıfkı did not want to be seen by him as the Great Leader's spokesperson.

Rıfkı wondered whether he would be able to save words in the same passionate manner in which he had purged them not so long ago. He walked towards the podium and began his defence of the word *hüküm* – judgement. The face of the Committee Leader, as he watched his old pupil, was filled with wonder.

"This word, *hüküm*, is often seen as Arabic-rooted," Rıfkı said. "Only last week, our dear linguist friend Yusuf Ziya had demanded that it be purged from language. But now, new evidence has emerged that shows that *hüküm* is among the purest words Turkish has ever had." Rıfkı took out a little paper from his jacket pocket and read the little paragraph inscribed on it: "Now, according to my research, ancient Turks had this word, *ök*, that they used to describe intellect. This word was often written as *ük*. As for *üm* you must all be aware how it had been used by ancient Turks as a building suffix. Together those two words, *ük* and *üm* form judgement, *hüküm*, which stands for the judgement of the intellect, the very meaning of *hüküm*! Therefore it would be absurd to purge this most Turkish of words from our language."

"What about the Arabic root hukm," the Committee Leader asked in a perplexed voice. "Is it not a more rational explanation to see the connection between the Arabic hukm and our *hüküm* and conclude that the latter is a variation of the former?"

"It is an explanation which, I have to say, reflects an *outre* approach to our language," Rıfkı said, "this is an approach that we need to leave behind... I am calling all committee members to consider the possibility that this combination of the completely Turkish *ük* and *üm* words might have predated that word's purportedly Arabic roots. If Turks have predated Arabs then what on earth can be more natural than our words predating theirs?" These words were followed by a murmur that filled the committee room and spiralled out from the doors.

When Rıfat stepped outside and used the zigzag road to reach the garden two hours later, Abdülkadir smiled at him.

"That was a good speech," he said. "A very good one indeed. And yet, I don't think anyone believed in what you said. Everyone knows that *hüküm* is Arabic. But don't worry, you have just saved judges and lawyers from the toil of changing the language in all their legal documents to make sure they use the new words."

"I was surprised that the Committee Leader did not insist on the Arabic connection."

"I don't think he could, my dear Rıfkı," Abdülkadir said before lighting a cigarette. "People say that the Minister of Justice had contacted him this morning and urged him to save *hüküm* even if you failed to defend it appropriately."

* * *

May 16, 2015. In the Court of Purity. From The Guardian

An Egyptian court has sentenced the ousted president Mohamed Morsi to death for his part in a mass jailbreak in 2011.

The verdict . . . was announced on Saturday in a Cairo court where Morsi was also facing charges of espionage. As is customary in passing capital punishment, the death sentence on Morsi and more than 100 others will be referred to the country's top Muslim theologian, or mufti, for his non-binding opinion.

Morsi, Egypt's first freely elected president, was ousted by the military in July 2013 after days of mass street protests by Egyptians demanding that he be removed because of his divisive policies.

His overthrow triggered a government crackdown on the Muslim Brotherhood movement, to which he belongs, in which hundreds of people have died and thousands have been imprisoned.

In May 2014, Morsi's successor, the former military chief Abdel Fatah al-Sisi, secured a landslide victory in Egypt's presidential elections.Before Saturday's sentencing, Morsi was already serving a 20-year term on charges linked to the killing of protesters outside a Cairo presidential palace in December 2012.

Defendants in both trials were brought into the caged dock on Saturday ahead of the verdict. "We are free revolutionaries, we will continue the march," they chanted.

Morsi was not brought in, but his co-defendant and Brotherhood leader, Mahmud Badie, was present, wearing the red uniform of those convicted to death after a previous sentence.

* * *

One day in 2015, an Egyptian judge woke up from a terrible nightmare in the green-coloured bedroom of an old Cairo mansion. For what felt like an interminable length of time he dreamt about a court of law filled with dozens of words looking at him with an expression of terrible desperation on their ink-black faces.

In the dream, he was a linguist to whom was given the power to purge or preserve words. The words were placed inside large metal cages at the centre of the courtroom. He could see their shapes and curves; their sick-looking vowels reached out from the cages and their silent consonants were visible from the podium where he sat. Their voices, in contrast, was incomprehensible to him – just an Oriental-sounding murmur filling the room and spiralling out from the cage, spelling out a message that was inaudible but no doubt addressed to him.

From behind the group of those words the dreamer discerned a word, الْحُرُوف العَرَبِيَّة, who eyed him with an intensity that sent shivers down his spine. Written with blindingly bright red letters, this was certainly a word of previous, freshly lost authority. The dreamer looked at this glowing prisoner in awe and fear and felt, on his shoulders, the responsibility of deciding the fate of him – whether the word should be saved or perish was entirely left to him. But before he could say or do anything, guards appeared in four corners of the court room.

They approached the cage and entered it.
They brought the red-coloured prisoner out and placed a piece of cloth around his head.

And then they took the word away. ⊗

Illustrations by Molly Crabapple

***Kaya Genç** is a Turkish novelist and journalist, based in Istanbul*

***Molly Crabapple**'s Drawing Blood (Harper Collins) is out in December*

HARMONIA-LYRA

Send in the clowns

44(03): 102/107 | DOI: 10.1177/0306422015605734

Brazilian journalist **Tuane Roldão** decided to investigate theatre in her hometown during the military dictatorship and discovered a darkly humorous play that was abandoned before its first performance. **Ana Minozzo** speaks to her about secrecy and censorship, and translates an extract of the play into English for the first time

WHEN JOURNALIST TUANE Roldão tried to ask her grandmother about how life was in her hometown of Joinville during Brazil's military dictatorship, the conversation was shut down. "I don't know what that is. That did not happen here," she would always insist.

Such a response was not uncommon, Roldão discovered, as she set about investigating the period from 1964 to 1985, when secretive torture and murder were rife. As an avid theatregoer, Roldão decided to focus her research on the town's arts scene and its censorship. The resulting book Acanhado, which translates as Sheepish, mixes reportage with interviews and extracts of previously unpublished plays.

In her lifetime, 24-year-old Roldão has seen Joinville, in the southern state of Santa Catarina, flourish to offer some of highest living standards in the country and an ever-growing arts scene, which includes one of the world's largest annual dance festivals →

LEFT: Harmonia Lyra, an arts venue in Joinville, a city in southern Brazil known for music, theatre and ballet

Credit: Fundação Turistica de Joinville

ABOVE: Brazilian playwright Miraci Deretti

→ and the only branch of the Bolshoi Ballet Academy outside Russia.

The industrial town was founded on immigration (predominantly German and Italian), and has a population known for being hard-working and reserved. This, said Roldão, meant that a lot of what was going on during the regime was never openly discussed and even less of what happened during the regime was documented.

"For a lot of people, nothing changed. They carried on with their routines, carried on working, studying, raising their kids," she explained.

While researching the arts scene, she heard interviewees repeatedly mention Os Palhaços (The Clowns), a play written by Miraci Deretti in 1968, which was intended to run at a local social club but was never publicly performed. The play was a victim of unofficial censorship, which saw creative people and thinkers "advised" they were better off keeping ideas to themselves. As Roldão said, psychological pressure that was often more devastating to projects than any official letter from the authorities.

In the play, Deretti, who was a Catholic seminary dropout, used clowns as his primary characters. The piece is full of subtle jokes and acidic language, and demonstrates a deep resentment towards dominating institutions, including the church and the military government.

"According to him, we are all clowns for allowing this exploitation to happen," Roldão said. "He also highlights the problems of hunger and extreme poverty, the relationship between employee and employer, the censorship of Protestants, and the individualism and egotism of human beings."

The play – an extract of which has been translated into English below for the first time – was finally performed in Joinville in 2008. Deretti died in 2009. In 2012, the Brazilian government founded the Comissão da Verdade (Truth Commission) to shine a light on the era's crimes. The board is currently investigating alleged murders from the period, but a military-era amnesty means there will be no trials.

The Clowns
by Miraci Deretti

CLOWN IX Jeez, son! Don't talk like that! God will punish you!

CLOWN III God ... this ain't got anything to do with God! This is all coming from those priests. God! God!

This is not God! This troublemaking God is an invention of those priests!

MEANWHILE, ON THE RADIO: Communism is creating more victims all the time! Communism is the root of all evils in the modern world! Communism, this perfidious and atheist doctrine, only Christ can defeat it!

CLOWN III Which Christ?! The one I know looks more like he's with the communists than with you, sir!

CLOWN II Brazil only creates and incubates clowns! Clowns proliferate in geometric progression! Brazil already had enough clowns to start exporting them

----

CLOWN III I would actually just like to win a few million! The day I get 30 million ... I ... will get lots of blacks to move their arses! I've got the money! Arrest me! You see! Who wins the lottery? Only the rich! A rich man is skint ... and what does he do? He goes to the bank: "Sir, fetch me five millions?!"

CLOWN II Subversive! World-repairing lunatic! Propagandist! Are you going to quit this argument or not? Just so you know you're starting to be annoying and you may end up getting yourself into trouble!

CLOWN I Go away, you professional ass-licker! Is this a democracy or a clownery?

CLOWN III It is a democracy with subtle dumb-ocratic tendencies!

CLOWN II The same faces, the same banks, the same people going down the same way

CLOWN VII Stop nagging, guys! Stop nagging me! You act as if you were born here! You can't see anyone relaxed without sticking your nose in!

CLOWN III Hold on a minute, now you have offended me! I am from here and I do not accept you bad-mouthing my homeland!

CLOWN I Well, you are one of the bearable ones. If only this land had more people like you, it would be a paradise!

CLOWN VIII Do you know the land where one can't be intelligent because the boss is dumb →

→ and he doesn't want to be over-shadowed in the shadow ... where a lad who owns a bar with three employees thinks he is the king of the world and has the right to control his employees' private lives ...

CLOWN II For all of this I keep saying:

Where there's a will, there's a way, my Brazilian people,

We can fix anything up with *jeitinho*[1]

No one will starve in Brazil,

Because there is always a *farofa*[2] with some fish!

If I'm living in a fixed-up shack,

Why do I need anything better if I am rarely going to sleep?

I have a serenade for my good friends

Life is good, I am better, I'm in Brazil!

All my offspring are going to be Brazilian

From a young age they will know how to live life...

Nobody works, because what do we get from it?

It's better just to find a way to get going!"

CLOWN X And the six-year-old little girl ... I saw her turn her sad little face to her mother and say: "Mother! Today we have nothing, right? So I will go to sleep!" Today we have nothing ... I thought it was the television! Or the radio. I thought it was a dessert. No! Today we have NOTHING ...There is nothing ... So I will go to sleep ... And I also went to sleep ... I forgot ... And you will also go to sleep ...

- - - - - - - - - - - - - - - - - - - -

CLOWN II And the clown found love!

CLOWN I He found out that those stories that say: "And they lived happily ever after ..."

CLOWN II Are only truthful when both people are ...

CLOWN I Me and myself!

CLOWN II But he found that horrible!

CLOWN I It is repugnant.

CLOWN II A huge clownery!

CLOWN I But men say that's what life is like! I only actually love ...

CLOWN II Myself ... And the clown thought that this way ...

CLOWN I Life is a stupid deal

- - - - - - - - - - - - - - - - - - - -

CLOWN I I became a clown! I really enjoy theatre. I enjoy dramatic scenes! I enjoy appearing in front of the spectators with that heroic, indecipherable look of one who has felt emotions more tragic than the human mind could possibly imagine. I enjoy looking at the audience, with that fantastic expression, capable of moving a heart of stone. Because I am a clown.

Translation and introduction by Ana Minozzo

Translation notes
1. Jeitinho: Brazilian expression denominating a national characteristic of being street-smart and getting away with anything. It can be either positive or negative.
2. Farofa: Brazilian-style manioc flour, toasted and flaked.

***Tuane Roldão** is a journalist, based in Joinville, Brazil. She is the author of Acanhado: Teatro em Joinville Durante a Ditadura Militar (Sheepish: Theatre in Joinville during the Military Dictatorship, Design Editora, 2014)*

LEFT: Writer Mikhail Zoshchenko picking apples from a street vendor

Credit: AKG/RIA Nowosti

Poetic portraits

44(03): 109/114 | DOI: 10.1177/0306422015605735

Russian poet **Marina Boroditskaya** introduces a **Lev Ozerov** poem, never published before in English, about comic writer Mikhail Zoshchenko, a man once denounced as an enemy of Soviet literature

LEV OZEROV'S BOOK of poems Portraits Without Frames, it seems to me, has no counterpart in Russian poetry. The author concocted such an inimitable mixture of the lyric and the epic that the very matter-of-factness of his tone makes me want to cry.

It feels right that this cycle of poems, never well-known, almost forgotten, has "popped out" just now. Somehow, poems always know when to surface. Could there be a better time for reading the poem about Varlam Shalamov (the Russian writer and poet sent to the Gulag) than now, when Stalin has been called "an effective manager" in a school history book? Shalamov, the great writer, back from the Gulag but still carrying all his belongings with him in a sack, keeping a palm under his chin while eating bread, so that not a crumb is lost... Could there be a better time for reading the poem about Shmuel Halkin, the Soviet Yiddish poet, than now, when the Russian parliament is considering whether they should excise War and Peace and other "over-complicated literature" from the secondary school curriculum? Halkin wrote poetry in Yiddish, but there was no paper for him in the Gulag, and when his memory had been exhausted, another prisoner who knew the language volunteered to memorise poems for him. When Halkin died, not long after his release, his "walking manuscript" found the family and dictated all he remembered of Halkin's last poems.

Poems surface when we most need them as an antidote – when the official lies concentrate dangerously in the atmosphere.

This poem about Mikhail Zoshchenko is one of my favourites. It is a highly realistic piece – every detail is recognisable – and at the same time it is pure magic. Reading it is like being present at a seance – with the poet as medium. I can feel Ozerov's shocked, almost fascinated disgust at the guffawing audience when he sees it through Zoshchenko's eyes and then cries out to Breughel and Goya. I can feel Zoshchenko's sadness – the heaviness, the enormousness of it.

And I can feel an overwhelming guilt that is my own. I was not born under Stalin, I was not there when Zoshchenko's friends and acquaintances crossed to the other side of the street, scared to be seen greeting him. But somehow it is my fault too.

I do not know how Ozerov managed to create such an impressionistic picture with his crude realistic strokes and colours. But the impression is deep.

© Marina Boroditskaya

***Marina Boroditskaya** is a Russian poet*

On Mikhail Zoshchenko

By Robert Chandler

Mikhail Zoshchenko (1895–1958) is best known for the comic short stories he wrote in the late 1920s. These were hugely popular; 700,000 copies of his books were sold in 1926–7 alone. Zoshchenko also won the admiration of other writers, from Maksim Gorky to Osip Mandelstam. In 1946 he was denounced as an "enemy of Soviet literature" and expelled from the Writers' Union. After this he wrote little of value. Zoshchenko' stories perfectly capture the texture of everyday life in Soviet Russia: the inescapable bureaucracy; the constant shortages of everyday necessities, especially living space; and people's strange eagerness to denounce one another. Zoshchenko is not only one of the funniest of Russian writers but also one of the most sober; no one is more aware of the harm carried out in the name of grand visions of progress. The harsh and cramped world of his stories is a paradoxically eloquent assertion of the importance of what is so strikingly absent from it: acts of kindness.

Lev Ozerov's "Portrait" of Mikhail Zoshchenko

This is how the story begins.
I had had my left eye operated on
in the clinic
of one of the fastest
and most furious
of our new businessmen,
a truly Soviet
caricature of a capitalist,
a man, I could see,
with an unerring
eye for commercial opportunity.
There were nine of us patients,
crowded into a small ward. I knew
everyone's name. We had already
talked about everything
there was
to talk about,
and there was nothing,
I think I can say,
we didn't know about one another.
We'd exhausted our supply
of jokes. Well-wishers
had ensured
that all of us
languishing in the hospital
had a clear grasp
of the system of bribes:
so much for a cataract,
so much for a glaucoma,
so much for a scratched lens,
so much for a detached retina –
each item in this list, of course,
more expensive
than the item before it.
And then there was a redoubtable lady,
an administrator who could have been
a grenadier guard, with a snowplough
of a bust and a baritone
that would have done her proud on stage.
She accepted payment
in cash
or in French cosmetics –
as long as the bottles
were not too small.

We were all feeling bored
and one of the other patients
said to me,
'You, probably, have some books.
You look like one of those…
intelligentsia. What's damaged
your eyes is books.
Get your friends to bring you some
so you can read to us.'
My friends
brought me some books.
I read a little Tolstoy:
The Sebastopol Stories.
'Not bad – but it's
ever so serious. And we've
all had enough of war.'
I tried Dostoevsky:
The Adolescent, Poor Folk.
'Not bad, but it's all
ever so serious. Enough
to make you start to cry.
Give us something
a bit simpler, something
that'll make us all laugh,
even just a little bit.'
And so I read them some Zoshchenko.
Everyone was transformed.
Everyone was reborn.
Laughter's more powerful than vitamins.
The roars of laughter made it difficult
to keep reading.
We knew joy
and a sense of community.
'Just what we need!' people were saying.
'That fellow knows his stuff!'
They were falling off mattresses.
Bandages were slipping off eyes.
In dashed Sister. 'What's going on
in here? I've never heard
such a racket. Stop all
this reading at once. You should
be ashamed of yourselves!'
I stopped reading. Everyone

ABOVE: A group of prisoners read a newspaper in a Russian gulag in 1932

went back to being bored.
Zoshchenko, once again,
was forbidden. Of course:
what else
could we have expected?
And so, instead of reading,
I talked to them about Zoshchenko.
My own thoughts and impressions.
Swarthy, quiet, timid. Brown eyes.
A man who had kept his counsel
among wheeler-dealers and their floozies,
among criminals and swindlers –
he knew them not from clever books
but from the life he'd led. He'd seen
enough – more than enough of them.
And he had learned
to keep his mouth shut.
He was a man like no one else.
His eyes had a wonderful glitter,
almost as if there were tears in them.
He seemed to me to be looking
somewhere into the depth of the soul,
as if the world lying outside
the soul were too much for him.
He'd been in the War,
he'd suffered concussion,
he'd been gassed. All this had left him
with heart problems. He had bred rabbits
and chickens. He had worked as a cobbler,
a policeman, an agent
for the Criminal Investigation Department.
This wealth of professions
had come in useful.
He'd got to know people.
Then it was time
to say goodbye to fun
and games, time for Zoshchenko
to start his real work.
How does it start –
the mad day, the mad life
of a writer? What whim,
what overwhelming force
presses a pen into some poor fellow's hand
and leads him down
through all of Dante's
twisting circles?

One day
I was walking
down Nevsky Prospekt
with Slonimsky – not the composer
but his father, the writer,
one of the 'Serapion Brothers'.
And there, coming towards us,
not far from the Anichkov Bridge
and Clodt's famous horses,
was Zoshchenko. Two writers,
two Serapions, two Mikhails,
two old friends. I was introduced.
'I've been wanting to meet you for years!'
I said breathlessly. Zoshchenko
said nothing. He seemed to be almost
pitying me. Had I said the wrong thing?
What was I to do? Best, I thought,
to hold my tongue. Which
I did. The two Mikhails
talked for a long time. And then,
as we were saying goodbye,
Zoshchenko said, 'I'm reading

PROFILE

Lev Ozerov: the poet and his history

By ROBERT CHANDLER

The term "man of letters" has a sadly old-fashioned ring. Lev Ozerov was a man of letters in the best sense of the words. He published books of poetry and criticism. He translated poetry from Yiddish, Hebrew, Ukrainian and Lithuanian. He taught courses in literary translation for around 50 years. He ran The Library of Oral Poetry, a series of more than 200 poetry readings, for around 10 years. As an editor, he was responsible for the publication or republication of many writers, including both Pasternak and Zabolotsky, who had suffered censorship and persecution. In 1946 he published a long poem about Babi Yar, the ravine on the outskirts of Kiev that was the site of the largest of the many Nazi massacres of Jews on Soviet soil.

Ozerov was always open-minded, never programmatic. His finest book, Portraits Without Frames, published after his death, comprises 50 accounts of meetings with important cultural figures, many – though not all – from the literary world. He writes with understanding and compassion not only about such great and courageous writers as Shalamov but also about such writers as Fadeyev, a Soviet literary boss who shot himself when Stalin's crimes, and his own complicity, began to be exposed under Khrushchev. The Serapion Brothers, mentioned in the poem, was a group of writers formed in Petrograd in 1921. Among its members were Victor Shklovsky, Mikhail Slonimsky and Zoshchenko himself.

Marina Boroditskaya writes with such grace, modesty and simplicity that it is easy to underestimate the breadth of her achievement. But she too, deserves the title of "(wo)man of letters".

Like Ozerov, she does all she can, in many ways, to support literature in all its manifestations. Poets she has translated include Chaucer (the first Russian translation of his Troilus and Criseyde), Shakespeare, Donne, Burns, Keats and Kipling. Children's writers she has translated included Hilaire Belloc, Eleanor Farjeon, A. A. Milne and Alan Garner. She has published at least 20 books of poetry for children and six for adults. She runs regular workshops for younger poets, both those writing for adults and those writing for children. She has for many years presented the Russian equivalent of BBC Radio Four's Poetry Please!, called The Literary First Aid Box, it is inspired by her belief that literature is the best medicine. A recent programme featured several poems by Ozerov. And like Ozerov, she has always, in her quiet, persistent way, been concerned with censorship and human rights. If Russia manages to avoid closing itself off from the world as it did in Ozerov's day, it will be thanks to people like her. ⊗

Credit: AKG images

this evening. A workers' club
in Vyborgskaya. Do come if you can!'
And he wrote down the address.

Slonimsky was doing something else,
but I went along. And I didn't regret it.
Zoshchenko and I arrived
together. Chance?
Sometimes chance is a bearer of gifts.
It was early. No one
to greet the writer. He invited me
backstage. We'd only just met
and there I was – in the role
of trusted friend. I was
all eyes, and I soon realised
that Zoshchenko was a lonely man
who hid this with great skill.
It was my lucky day:
The author, Zoshchenko,
reading his own work.
And me backstage, looking out
into the packed hall. Z. read

→

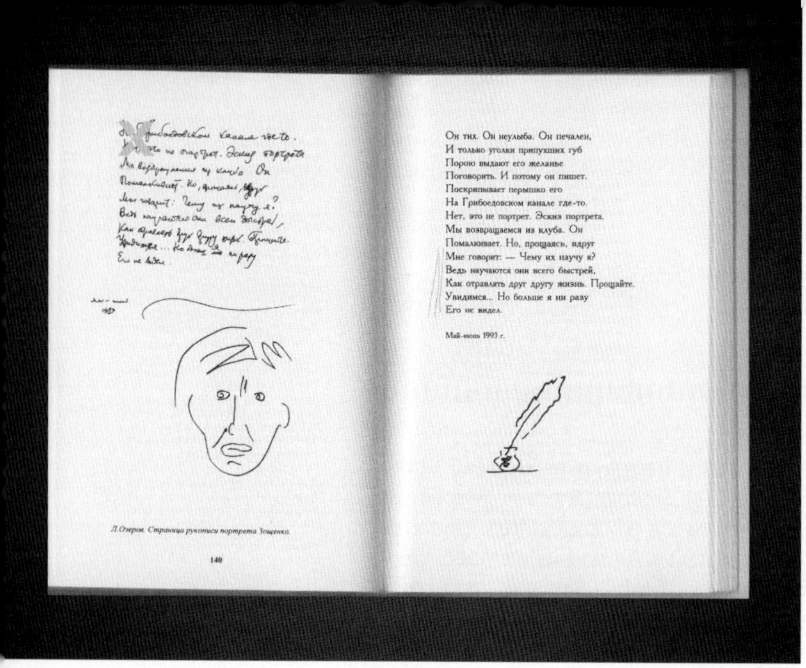
Он тих. Он неулыба. Он печален,
И только уголки припухших губ
Порою выдают его желанье
Поговорить. И потому он пишет.
Поскрипывает перышко его
На Грибоедовском канале где-то.
Нет, это не портрет. Эскиз портрета.
Мы возвращаемся из клуба. Он
Помалкивает. Но, прощаясь, вдруг
Мне говорит: — Чему их научу я?
Ведь научаются они всего быстрей,
Как отравлять друг другу жизнь. Прощайте.
Увидимся... Но больше я ни разу
Его не видел.

Май-июнь 1993 г.

Л.Озеров. Страница рукописи портрета Зощенко.

140

ABOVE: Drawings of Zoshchenko by Ozerov, published in the Russian edition of Portraits Without Frames

clearly, as if at ease,
as if simply chatting,
one to one, with individual listeners.
He read The Forked Object
and The Aristocratic Lady.
He sounded sad and thoughtful –
and the audience went wild.

They roared with laughter.
I saw mouths twisted into strange shapes;
I heard snorts, neighs and bleats.
One man was slapping his hand on his knee;
another kept turning his head
madly from side to side;
a third was trying to silence
someone mooing and weeping beside him.
A fourth was howling, head
thrown back. Where were you,
Breughel? O Goya,
where were you? I saw these things
with my own eyes.
And I saw thoughtful looks,
expressions of deep alarm;
I saw the shining faces of true
lovers of the word. And I saw
Zoshchenko, calm and pale,
retire back stage,
a little hunched, as if battered
by the waves – those rolling
breakers of applause.

'Why are they all laughing?'
he asked. 'I've been telling them
terrible things.' With a shrug
of despair he goes out again.
One more story. The story's creator
is swarthy, brown-eyed.
Quiet. Unsmiling. Sad.
And only now and then
do the corners of his slightly
swollen mouth betray
that he has something to say.
And so he writes, his pen
scratching away in some room
near the Griboyedov canal.
No, this is no portrait. Only
a first sketch. We leave the club.
He says nothing. But then,
as we're saying goodbye: 'What can I
teach them? All they ever learn,
and they learn it quicker and quicker,
is how to poison one another's lives.
Goodbye. See you soon.' But I
never
saw Zoshchenko again.

Translated and introduction by Robert Chandler

***Robert Chandler** is best known for his translations from Russian. These include: Alexander Pushkin's The Captain's Daughter; Vasily Grossman's Everything Flows, The Road and Life and Fate, and An Armenian Sketchbook; many works by Andrey Platonov; and Hamid Ismailov's novel The Railway, set in central Asia.*

His first article about Vasily Grossman, along with his translations of some brief extracts from Life and Fate, was published in Index on Censorship in the early 1980s

Index around the world

INDEX NEWS

44(03): 115/118 | DOI: 10.1177/0306422015605736

Max Goldbart rounds up Index's recent work and events, including a major comedy fundraiser and campaigning for rights in Azerbaijan

ABOVE: Comedian Frankie Boyle performing a set at Stand Up for Satire

Credit: Credit: Elina Kansikas

"TONIGHT, I AM going to reignite your faith in censorship," joked comedian Frankie Boyle at Stand Up for Satire, a night of comedy arranged by Index on Censorship to highlight the importance of protecting satire worldwide.

Hosted by Al "The Pub Landlord" Murray, the event at the Union Chapel in north London drew a sell-out crowd of 900, with performances from some of the biggest names in British and Irish comedy: Andrew Maxwell, Frankie Boyle, Kerry Godliman, Doc Brown, Gráinne Maguire and Shappi Khorsandi (host of Index's Freedom of Expression Awards in March).

Index has always championed comedians, satirists and cartoonists facing persecution around the world. To complement the event, a set of articles from the Index on Censorship magazine archive on censorship and comedy, including pieces by Milan Kundera and Rowan Atkinson, were re-published.

In July, Index joined with the Sabeen Mahmud Foundation to host a tribute to the murdered activist, in London. Sabeen Mahmud was the founder of The Second Floor, a coffee house and "community space for open dialogue" in Karachi, Pakistan. She was killed by gunmen in April, after hosting a panel discussion on the missing people of Balochistan. Our joint event, Unsilencing Pakistan, took place in her honour.

British-Pakistani comedian Aatif Nawaz hosted the night of speakers and performers celebrating Sabeen's life and Pakistani culture. Childhood friends of Sabeen, including activist Ali Dayan Hasan and novelist Kamila Shamsie, spoke, and there were also talks on the state of free speech in Pakistan by The New York Times correspondent Declan Walsh, and Tehmina Kazi, from British Muslims for Secular Democracy.

Also in July, the summer issue of Index on Censorship magazine, themed on academic freedom, was launched at Birkbeck, University of London, with a debate entitled Silenced on Campus. Panellists included Greg Lukianoff, president of America's Foundation for Individual Rights in Education; Lord Ken Macdonald, the ex-director of public prosecutions and Liberal Democrat life peer; journalist Julie Bindel, Nicola Dandridge chair of Universities UK, and blogger and spoken-word artist Siana Bangura. Chaired by Index CEO Jodie Ginsberg, the debate explored no-platforming, safe spaces, trigger warnings and the new UK Counter-Extremism Bill, which looks set to further restrict free speech on British campuses by introduc-

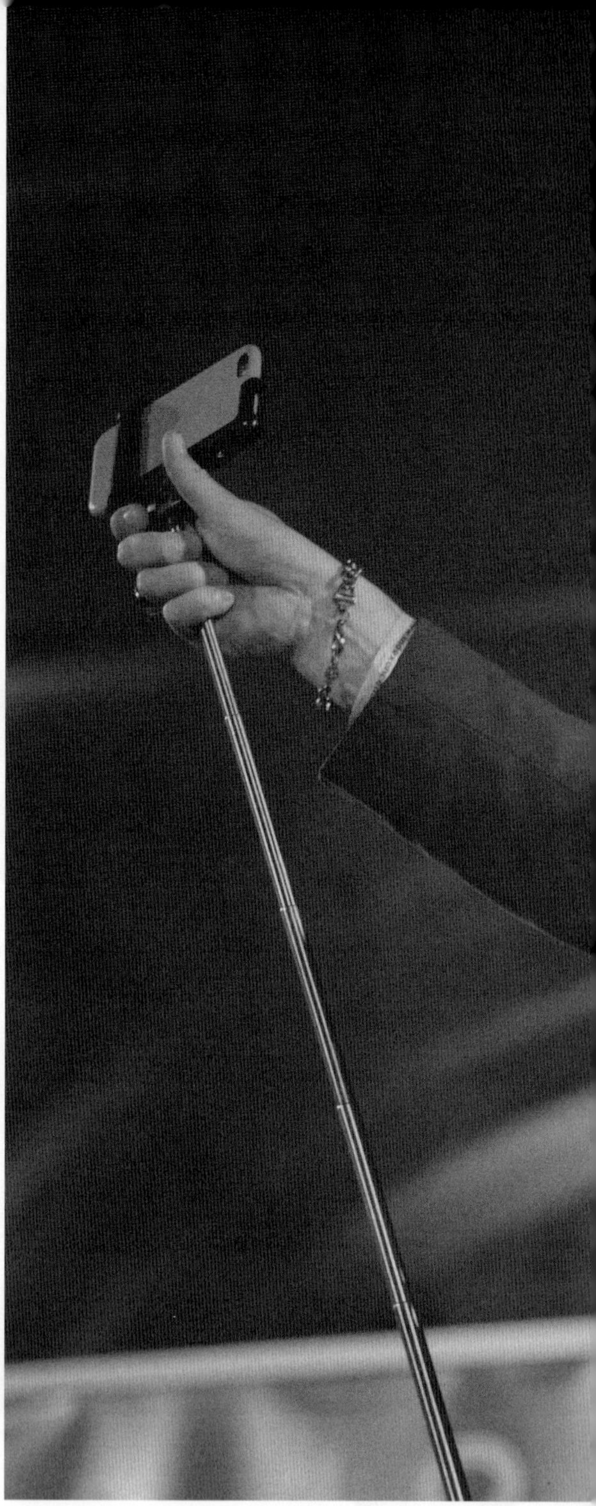

Credit: Elina Kansikas

ing measures aimed at targeting "extremist" rhetoric.

Index helped organise a protest outside the Azerbaijani embassy in South Kensington on 12 June, the day of the European Games' opening ceremony in Azerbaijan. It happened just after The Guardian's chief sports correspondent Owen Gibson, representatives from Amnesty International and an activist from Platform London were denied entry to the country for the duration of the games. The inaugural European Games took place in Azerbaijan in June, which Index used to draw people's attention to the many censored and imprisoned journalists in the country. These include human rights activists Leyla and Arif Yunus, human rights lawyer Intigam Aliyev, pro-democracy campaigner Rasul Jafarov and investigative journalist Khadija Ismayilova.

Index senior advocacy officer Melody Patry said: "Index continues to follow closely the cases of imprisoned journalists and activists. As Azerbaijan prepares to host other →

ABOVE: Comedian Al Murray poses with a selfie stick at Stand Up for Satire

→ sporting events, Index remains active in the Sport for Rights campaign and will continue to denounce the ongoing repression of those who express dissent, expose corruption or support human rights."

Other recent events included a discussion on artistic censorship in repressive regimes at the National Centre for Early Music in Walmgate in June. The panel, chaired by Index's associate arts producer Julia Farrington, included Iranian sisters and former Index on Censorship Freedom of Expression award winners Mahsa and Marjan Vahdat, both of whom are artists and singers who strongly advocate freedom of expression.

Stand Up For Satire drew a sell-out crowd of 900, with performances from some of the biggest names in British and Irish comedy

At Leeds Big Bookend festival, Index on Censorship magazine's editor Rachael Jolley led a debate entitled The new civility: are religious freedom and freedom of speech intertwined?

On the panel were Yorkshire Evening Post assistant features editor Chris Bond; local imam Qari Muhammad Asim; and author and Index contributor Anthony Clavane.

And at Wilderness in Oxfordshire, festival goers packed a large marquee for an Index debate on cartooning and offence. The Independent's cartoonist Dave Brown; Nigerian cartoonist Tayo; Prospect Magazine's Sameer Rahim; and Index chairman, journalist David Aaronovitch all took part.

Index on Censorship now has a new youth advisory board, a global network of free expression enthusiasts aged between 18 and 25. There were over 40 applications to become part of the July-to-December roster. The appointed group of nine, hailing from Bosnia, the Netherlands, South Africa, India, the UK and the US, will now meet virtually, via Google Hangouts, once a month. As well as acting as global Index ambassadors, they will also research a variety of written and multimedia news features, which will be published on the Index website.

Finally, Index on Censorship has become a founder member of the Leipzig-based European Centre for Press and Media Freedom. The centre also brings together the European Federation of Journalists and Russian Mass Media Defence Centre, along with academic institutions from around Europe. Its aim is to address media freedom and violations in EU member states and beyond. Index CEO Jodie Ginsberg said, "Index is thrilled to be part of this initiative because of its potential to increase the impact of all media freedom campaigns in the region." Index's own Mapping Media Freedom project has now verified and published around 900 reports of assaults on journalistic free expression from more than 40 countries, and has recently been expanded to cover Russia, Belarus and Ukraine. Hannah Machlin, project officer for Mapping Media Freedom, said: "In light of the draconian measures against independent journalism within the former Soviet Union, the project is expanding to cover new countries."

The project uses two methods to gather reports, crowd-sourcing and Index's 17 correspondents around the region, and then records attacks on journalists. Details are factchecked before being added to the map. The team will also offer legal advice and support to journalists who request it as well as offering digital security training. ⊗

***Max Goldbart** is editorial assistant at Index on Censorship Magazine and is currently finishing a master's degree in magazine journalism from Cardiff University's School of Journalism, Media and Cultural Studies*

A matter of facts

END NOTE

44(03): 119/120 | DOI: 10.1177/0306422015605737

Vicky Baker looks at the rise of fact-checking organisations being used to combat misinformation, from the UK to Argentina and South Africa

EVERY WEDNESDAY AT noon, the British prime minister takes to the floor of the House of Commons to answer, or evade, questions from members of Parliament. Every Wednesday, at the same time, a small group of factcheckers turn up their television in a central London office, and gets ready for action. They are poised to live-tweet corrections or queries, and to investigate new claims or surprise statistics through their website. On the wall are posters with slogans such as "Spurious makes us curious".

FullFact, the UK's only independent factchecker, was established in 2010, but 2015 has been its breakthrough year. During the UK general election, it staffed an 18-hour-a-day "rapid-reaction centre", made possible by a crowd-funding campaign. It responded to queries from the public, and from journalists, as well as checking manifestos and speeches. One of the team's proudest moments was when they contacted BBC's Newsnight mid-broadcast and a correction appeared before the programme ended.

"It seems like we are capturing a global zeitgeist," Fullfact's director, Will Moy, told Index. "I'm not sure if it's [due to] a growing sense of distrust or because the internet makes it easier to factcheck and compare primary sources. Maybe it's a search for authenticity? We're definitely tapping into something."

Index visited FullFact in the same week of July as the Global Fact-Checking Summit, held at City University, London, and attended by 70 factcheckers and academics from around the world.

Among those represented was Africa-Check.org, a non-profit factchecker running since 2012, based in the journalism department of the University of the Witwatersrand in Johannesburg. The project was devised by the AFP Foundation (the non-profit arm of the international news agency), with seed-funding from Google. It also operates in Nigeria and Senegal (in French), and next year will open a division in Kenya.

"In Africa, reliable and accurate information is scarce," Peter Cunliffe-Jones, its director and a former foreign correspondent, told Index. "Factchecking is a difficult thing to do. But the popular reaction has been great – from readers and also from media houses, who have taken our reports and interviewed our researchers."

AfricaCheck recently challenged inflated claims about immigration to South Africa – repors that were fuelling xenophobia amid concerns about immigrants supposedly flooding the country. "The New York Times reported there were five million immigrants. The census figures are 2.2 million. We found no justification for this [higher] figure. Nobody has been able to explain where these other 3 million people have come from," said Cunliffe-Jones. The BBC, Reuters, the Mail Online and various South African media had also used the unverified figure.

"But we are not an anti-media organisation," he added. "We don't want to feed →

RIGHT: Independent factcheckers Full Fact provided an 18-hour-a-day "rapid-reaction centre" during the 2015 UK general elections

→ into an idea that all media or all politicians are liars. If we dig into something and find out it is true, we say so."

The United States spearheaded the factchecking movement, with Factcheck.org operating since 2003 and PolitiFact.com, run by the Tampa Bay Times, since 2007. Yet Moy expressed a reservation about the US approach. He cited a blog post that FactCheck.org wrote about the 2008 US election, which said that more than 40 per cent of Americans believed falsehoods about both candidates' tax plans, and one in five falsely believed Barack Obama was a Muslim. Moy said: "[FactCheck.org] took that as evidence that they were doing the right thing [by exposing the ignorance]. We take that as evidence that something is not working."

FullFact, by contrast, focuses almost as much on the correction as the debunking, he said. One of its tasks involves trying to identify things that go wrong repeatedly. A success story has been convincing the Office for National Statistics to add a line to one of their regular press releases to explain what the statistics didn't mean – in order to halt the normal stream of misleading headlines. Although Moy says the ONS was reluctant and only agreed after watchdog intervention.

In Argentina, finding and disseminating reliable statistics is harder. Along with a highly polarised press, the country has a shambolic national-statistics office (Indec), which has been underestimating inflation for years.

Enter Chequeado, South America's first independent factchecking organisation. Like FullFact, it started in 2010 and has similarly expanded to around 10 staff.

Chequeado's director, Laura Zommer, said that although there was no shortage of information, the problem was circulating it. "Often, the individuals have information that contradicts a minister, but they aren't going to come out and say it publicly, because they are scared, or because they don't want the confrontation. Part of our work is to generate a platform that is neutral. We want people to feel able to come to us with information," she said. Since Chequeado began, more Latin American factchecking organisations have appeared, including Uruguay's uycheck.com and Mexico's El Sabueso (run by AnimalPolítico.com).

Many of these new operations seem to share a focus on training, education and innovation. FullFact is working on an automated factchecking system, instantly noticing when claims have been checked before. Chequeado is creating new apps and smartphone alerts, to make factchecking more appealing and user-friendly.

"We're not going to let our campaign be dictated by factcheckers," said an aide to the US presidential candidate Mitt Romney in 2012, raising eyebrows around the world. But ignore the factcheckers at your peril. They look set to become much more powerful players. ⊗

Vicky Baker is the deputy editor of Index on Censorship magazine